From the Southland

Copyright © 2011 by Thomas Lux

Edited by Katie Chaple
Book design by HSDesigns

Marick Press
P.O. Box 36253
Grosse Pointe Farms, Michigan 48236
www.marickpress.com

Printed and bound in the United States

Library of Congress Cataloging-in-Publication Data
Lux, Thomas
From the Southland
ISBN 978-1-934851-37-1

From the Southland

(NONFICTION)

Thomas Lux

OTHER TITLES BY THOMAS LUX:

Memory's Handgrenade, 1972
The Glassblower's Breath, 1976
Sunday, 1979
Half Promised Land, 1986
The Drowned River, 1990
Split Horizon, 1994
The Blind Swimmer: Selected Early Poems 1970–1975, 1996
New and Selected Poems 1975–1995, 1997
The Street of Clocks, 2001
The Cradle Place, 2004
God Particles, 2008
Child Made of Sand, 2012

All of these articles appeared first, in slightly different form, in the *San Diego Reader*. Special thanks to the editor and founder of the *Reader*, James Holman, and to Heather Goodwillie for her infinitely patient copyediting.

For Judith Moore (1940–2006),
    in memoriam and in gratitude

Contents

Judith
13

The Farm in the Valley
15

The Red Book
32

Tiny Creatures
52

The Bridge
69

Oh Ducks
84

Eat Fire
102

Suffer The Little Children
118

Hyp-No-Tized
142

The Russian Poet of San Diego
159

3 A.M.
177

We Weep For Our Strangeness
192

Norman Ottomar Lux
213

JUDITH

Judith Moore called me in the early spring of 1995 while I was living temporarily in Laguna Beach, CA, and teaching at UC Irvine for a semester. Judith was familiar with my poems and from some of them deduced I'd grown up on a dairy farm. She wanted me to write an article for the *San Diego Reader*, a weekly newspaper, on one of the last remaining dairymen in San Diego County, a man named Pete Verboom. He lived in Pauma County, only about forty to fifty miles from Laguna, but an entirely different world.

She said the article had to be at least 6,000 words long. Then she said something I hadn't heard before in my writing life: The *Reader* would pay me $3,000. I'd published six full-length books of poetry by then, four of them with a major house, and I'd made maybe twice that much money from their combined royalties. I said to Judith: "Sure." To myself I said: "How hard can this be?"

A few days later, I said to myself: "I don't have the slightest idea how to do this!" I visited Mr. Verboom's farm for a few days—watched him and his brother pull some calves, put on the rubber boots, interviewed him and his wife. Mr. Verboom gave me a journal that his father had written on the voyage from post-war Holland to a new life in the USA, an aid to the assignment.

I tried to write the article—it was a miserable mess; awkward, dopey sentences. I had no idea. Nonfiction is a craft, a narrative craft unto itself, and even though I've always read a great deal of it, I had no idea how to *write* it.

And over and over again Judith helped. I was back in the East, living in Boston (where my daughter was) and commuting to New York (where I taught). Judith gave me tips: "The people you interview write a lot of the article for you. Interview them, quote them." She cajoled me. She encouraged me. She got draconian on my ass. I remember once saying something like: "So you're giving me permission to…and she said: "No, I'm *telling* you to!" She beat me over the head for using too many passive verbs, the same thing for which I beat my poetry students over the head. We'd often talk for two to three hours—about this article and others that followed—at a time. (Note: Though an editor at the *San Diego Reader*, Judith lived in Berkeley.) She spent a huge amount of energy trying to help me write decent prose sentences.

We became friends during these talks too, telling each other our sad and our happy stories. She was my teacher and she was my friend.

Judith was a wonderful writer. I loved her long and beautifully (a word, as an adjective or an adverb, she forbid me to use!) written series on the 50s San Diego mob figure, Frank Bompensiero. I hope these articles get published in a book* someday. They should have been in the running for a Pulitzer. I loved her book *Never Eat Your Heart Out*. I loved her last book, *Fat Girl*. She was just beginning to get major recognition for her own work. I was delighted when she got a Guggenheim Fellowship before she became ill. We must have talked and (later) emailed for hundreds of hours in the nearly ten years I knew her. Judith Moore was my friend. I loved her. We never met in person.

(*It has: *A Bad, Bad Boy*, Reader Books, 2009)

The Farm in the Valley

"There is a valley is the oldest story."
—Bill Knott

Pete (Pieter Johannes) Verboom, owner of Pauma Valley Dairy, a family operation milking a thousand cows in the town of Pala, was only a few months old when his homeland, Holland, was invaded and occupied by the Nazis in the spring of 1940. The first five years of his life reverberated with jackboots, shortages, fear, etc. The winter of 1944–45 was known as the Hunger Winter—about 20,000 Dutch citizens died of starvation. The Nazis stole about 100,000 Dutch bicycles to melt down and reuse the metal. Even today, a German tourist in Amsterdam might hear someone yell: "Give me back my bicycle!" On the day I visited his farm, he didn't mention any of this. I got a lot of information from his father's diary of his family's voyage to America. They left Antwerp on November 22, 1946 and docked in Los Angeles on January 10, 1947.

Pete Verboom's father William (Willem), a dairy farmer, was thirty-four years old, married to Nell (Neeltje) De Bruin Verboom, three years younger, and they had three children: Gladys (Klassje), the translator of her father's diary and ten at the time, Martin (Maarten) seven, and Pete, six.

The ship, the S.S. Duivendijk, a freighter, once belonged to the German Navy and was given to Holland as part of war reparations. It was not the Queen Mary but neither did the Verbooms travel steerage class. Mr. Verboom and his sons shared a cabin with "a farmer from Leidsedam, by name of Jansen. His 19-year-old daughter, Henny, would share a cabin with my wife and daughter. *We were lucky because farmers by farmers usually works out the best.*" (Italics mine.)

The diary is articulate, specific, quotidian, and contains much you would expect: Rounds of seasickness, boredom, difficulties of living in confined spaces with others, particularly strangers, a sense of loss of the old world, and anxiety regarding the new. Moments of wonder occur, like this, eight days out: "Six A.M. I awaken and look out the porthole and say to Mr. Jansen there is another ship sailing alongside. So we get out of bed and go on deck to see it better. We discover that what I had thought to be running lights of a ship were really two big stars, so big and so bright like we have never seen before. Back in the hall we met Mrs. Zyls with a bedpan in her hand; we had a good laugh and crawled back into bed."

On December 7, five years after Japan's attack on Pearl Harbor, the ship docks in Curaçao for cargo. Curaçao was part of the Dutch West Indies: "Everyone is very pro-Holland." After lunch on board, Willem and two other passengers (not the children) decide to explore the port city of Willemstad, the island's capital. They have one dollar among them. It's hot. They're thirsty, but a single beer costs seventy-five cents. Farming, dairy farming in particular, is never far from his mind, even on this tropical island: "The cows are so skinny, although it is no wonder with the condition of their pastures." They continue their adventure, hitching rides, walking, and, at one point, because of their thirst, they consider entering a soda bottling plant. The other two men decide to go in and wrangle for something to drink. Willem is reluctant: "Mr. Jansen and Rinus wanted to go in, but I was holding back because I felt like a beggar."

With that sentence I knew something important about this man that I would notice in his son, Pete Verboom, when I first spoke to him nearly forty-nine years later, after he had been on this farm in Pauma Valley for thirty years: A prodigious capacity for work and bedrock integrity.

The three men make their way to a Dutch merchant, a Captain Vrengdehill, who gives them glasses of ice-cold lemonade. When leaving, they try to pay but there's no charge. Willem adds: "You could see he did it completely out of hospitality and not because he felt sorry for us. We thanked him profusely and he left us with good advice buttoned in our ears: 'Keep your eyes open—be willing to use your hands and you will have a good chance of success in the world.' He said it sincerely, like a father to a son."

The rest of the voyage was uneventful. They stop in Columbia where they sail up the Magdalena River to Barranquilla. On the way he writes: "A dead cow drifts by; it probably went one step too far into the river." They are delayed in Panama for nearly three weeks for repairs. More excursions ashore, this time the whole family, visiting the local USO for movies, music. There's one last stop in Guatemala for a cargo of bananas.

Gladys Verboom De Boer has the following paragraph as part of her brief introduction to her translation of her father's diary:

> The reader must keep in mind that the amazement shown at and the frequent references made to such everyday items as bananas, oranges, cigarettes and automobile traffic are the direct result of the scarcity or non existence of those things because of the Second World War spent under German occupation in Holland.

The entry for January 7, 1947 starts: "Beautiful weather, a sunny summer day. We're eating bananas, bananas, bananas! We are now in the Gulf of California and on the last phase of our trip." Three days later: "Finally, in the distance, we see the lights of San Pedro, the harbor of Los Angeles." The diary closes with: "There comes an end to everything, also as you can see, this journey from Holland to the United States of America."

About a month short of forty-nine years later, I visit Pete Verboom, his wife Lani, his brother Martin, and a few of his dairymen on his farm in Pauma Valley. Pauma Valley is about forty miles northeast of San Diego. You reach it by driving north on Route 15 to Route 76 East. Very quickly, you enter the narrow opening to the valley. Cleveland National Forest borders the whole area on the west. The road follows a small river, the San Luis Rey, nearly dry in early December, but a serious flashflood threat (I learn later). It doesn't look like dairy country: No rolling pastures dotted with cow-pies. (Cow-flop was the colloquial of my time and place, which was Western Massachusetts in the 1950s.) I stopped at a farm stand and learned Pete Verboom's property was only another quarter mile down the road where the valley bottom widened a bit. The first thing one sees is one of the two milking barns, very close to the road. A worn sign reads "Pauma Valley Dairy, Pete Verboom, Owner." Most of the milk barns, workers' houses, outbuildings, etc. are painted pale green. Just past the milking barn are the first of the large feedlots. The cows live, eat, sleep in these enclosures, trudging back and forth twice a day to be milked. These corrals are dry, brown, dusty, and bare but for the cows, who stand around, heavy-headed, in twos or threes or singly. The Verbooms' small, ranch style house stands a little way up the opposite side of the valley, and across the above-mentioned river, which divides the property. Citrus groves dot the area, and a lot of avocado farms patch the mountainsides, but no other dairies. Once, this valley held four. Although California boasts over 3,000 dairy farms, making it the largest dairy farming state in the country, in San Diego County less than ten still operate.

 I spent most of my childhood, from age three to eighteen, living on a small family dairy farm in Massachusetts. My grandfather and uncle were the dairymen, milking only about thirty cows, a living in those days. My father was the milkman. Most of what I knew about dairy farming I'd forgotten, but occasionally I wrote about that life in poems:

COWS

Trochee, trochee, trochee—that's how

I heard them, the cows,
their beings, they walked
like that into the barn each night
and out again each morning after giving up their milk.
They were always eating, their heads down,
in field or barn,
eating grass or grain.
The field short cropped, lunar,
dotted with rocks,
cow-pies. Out of thirty, maybe three
or four you gave names
to: Bossy, Bessy. They were stupid,
not cute, and would not love or nuzzle you.
They went out in the morning and came back at dusk.
They didn't just hand it over,
their milk, but you could take it from them,
great foamy pails
emptied into vats
and sold for cash, all but one large blue pitcherful,
which stayed home
and which, when cold,
you poured atop a bowl of oatmeal
and ate through a thousand winters, every day
safe, tame, broken, and lost.

It wasn't easy setting up a day to visit Verboom's farm—once when we had agreed to talk on the phone to make arrangements for my visit, he was out on a tractor, towing a visitor who had taken a wrong turn into his watermelon patch and gotten stuck. Another time he canceled my visit because of a trip he had to make upstate. His two sons, Pete Jr., thirty-four, and Chris, thirty-two, live about a hundred miles north of Sacramento. Both of them are dairy farmers. They live and work on adjacent properties. His oldest daughter, Suzanne, married a dairy farmer and lives near her brothers. His youngest daughter, Julie, attends college at Point Loma Nazarene, but she wants to marry a dairyman, raise calves, live the farm life too. Her father told me this, and even though I am the father of a daughter myself and find it unwise to speak her mind for her, I did not feel it was wishful thinking on his part.

Pete Verboom is a big man, over six feet, broad-shouldered, barrel-chested. As he pointed out to me: Hauling around 170-pound bales of hay, leaning into 1,000-pound-plus animals to get them to move the way you want them to is better exercise than you can get at any health club. He was teased as a child by members of the S.S. Duivendijk's loading crew about his *vette bassie*—fat body. He's certainly not fat now, but he also clearly doesn't drink skim milk with his meals. His hand, when I first shook it in the still-dark early morning, was huge, strong, and warm. Unlike many farmers' hands I remember, his were not missing any fingers or parts of fingers. His features are unmistakably Dutch. I didn't see a picture of him as a child, but I bet he could have been on the paint can. In a wedding photo I saw of him at nineteen, he looks like a young Troy Donohue.

I noticed a row of rubber boots lined up outside his kitchen door and asked if I could borrow a pair for the day. I hadn't forgotten everything about dairy farming.

We drove down a steep hill to his calving pens on a battered three-wheel off-road vehicle. He has two corrals here. One for cows close to giving birth, another, adjacent, for cows *very* close to giving birth. In a year, nearly 2,000 calves are born on this farm. He cut the twine on bales of hay stacked in front of the fence and broke it up with a pitchfork. It surprised me to see the bales of hay bound with twine, not wire. The early hay baling machines used twine but then switched to wire. It turns out that wire sometimes contaminated the hay and bits of it got eaten by cows. To counteract this, cows were induced to swallow magnets. The pieces of metal would cling to the magnet, lodged in the cow's first stomach, and keep it from contaminating the cow's internal digestive and milk-making (more on this shortly) apparatus. It was eventually deemed safer and easier to go back to twine. Pete uses approximately 70,000 tons of hay a year. There are huge piles of it everywhere, mostly under open-sided sheds. Hay that gets wet can ignite under the right, or wrong, circumstances: Spontaneous combustion. It's the cause of most barn fires, a too-common farm disaster. Verboom had lost several thousand tons to a fire a few years earlier. A barn fire in my childhood killed over thirty cows and several horses.

BARN FIRE

It starts, somehow, in the hot damp
and soon the lit bales
throb in the hayloft. The tails
of mice quake in the dust,
the bins of grain, the mangers stuffed
with clover, the barrels of oats
shivering individually in their pale
husks—animate and inanimate: they know
with the first whiff in the dark.
And we knew, or should have: that day
the calendar refused its nail
on the wall and the crab apples hurling
themselves to the ground… Only moments
and the flames like a blue fist curl
all around the black. There is some
small blaring from the calves and the cows'
nostrils flare only once
more, or twice, above the dead dry
metal troughs… No more fat tongues worrying
the salt licks, no more heady smells
of deep green from silos rising now
like huge twin chimneys above all this.
With the lofts full there is no stopping
nor even getting close: it will rage until
dawn and beyond,—and the horses,
because they know they are safe there,
the horses run back into the barn.

We sat on some bales and began to talk. I asked specific questions. How many gallons of milk did he produce a day? Seven thousand, his cows all Holsteins, the most productive milk cows, all his milk strictly for drinking (not for cheese, etc.), all 1,000 head (except for a period before and after calving) milked twice a day, every day, each mass milking taking about five hours. A tanker truck comes each day to take the milk, which is sold to a wholesale milk dealer.

You have probably heard, at one time or another, that cows have four stomachs. The first three of these chambers (rumen, reticulum, and omasum) are probably derived from the esophagus. Millions of bacteria and protozoans live in the rumen and reticulum. When the cow eats (grass, grain, hay), the microbes begin to digest and ferment the food, breaking down the protein, starch, fats, and cellulose. The coarser, harder-to-digest material is periodically regurgitated as cud, chewed some more, and swallowed again. This is why cows often chew when they do not seem to be eating. This is one reason, I believe, they're so goddamned dumb-looking. Gradually, the products of this microbial action move into the cow's true or fourth stomach and intestine, called the abomasum, and further digestion and absorption takes place. A female calf, when born, is called a heifer calf, and becomes a heifer at about twenty-four to twenty-seven months when it is ready to mate and calve. It is this calving that stimulates the actual production of the milk. A cow cannot be milked until she has given birth. When she does, the calf is taken from her shortly thereafter. Just as a human female continues to produce milk as long as the child nurses, a cow continues to make and give milk as long as her nipples (udders) are stimulated, either by hand or by machine. When I was a child, my uncle, an expert at milking by hand, could angle a cow's udder and shoot a jet of milk right between the eyes of myself or my cousins. He got a laugh out of this, and so did we, but it was also a warning: Get too close to a cow and she's in a bad mood, she might kick you.

Verboom doesn't do the actual milking himself anymore—his dairymen do. His main hands-on job is pulling calves. Of all the calves born each year a fair percentage need help. His other main task is the business of farming, which is enormously complicated. A farmer, if he is to survive, has to be a good manager, like any businessman. Pete Verboom is the manager, CEO, foreman, overseer, the-buck-stops-here man of his business. If you think of farmers as rubes, rustics chewing on a piece of hay and opining about the weather: Don't. He has about thirty people working for him, one of whom is his brother, Martin, and some other hands, including several Mexican workers who are his primary dairymen. They live with their families on the property in ranch houses, none of which seem any smaller or much different than the Verbooms'. I saw several children on bicycles, playing, running along the dusty roads. This farm is their home. The children call him *Opa*: Grandpa. He and his family participate in the weddings, funerals, and holidays of his workers. He's fired only one man in thirty years, but I got the impression he does not tolerate slackers. Some of his hands have been with him over twenty-five years; sometimes a hand's son also comes to work for him.

It was about 7:30, now full light, and already quite warm. I asked him what he loved about his work.

> Verboom: I think for me the best time of the day is early in the morning when I'm out here by myself or my wife is with me. She's usually with me out here. Well, I'll set up the bales and she'll cut the twine, and it's time to talk, and that part, I would hate to lose that part.
>
> Int: And that's where you talk about your kids, your...?
>
> Verboom: Everything. Whatever—and it's so quiet down here in the mornings. Now you hear equipment start rolling, but in the early morning it's peaceful. And I love working with animals, and

a big part of my business is buying and selling and trading feed and cattle and calves. I love the trading part of it, the dealing. I love to trade.

He told me an anecdote about his two sons. They came to him in high school and told him they wanted to go into the dairy business. He said OK, but here's the deal: You both come to work for me for a few years to really learn the business, and you put two-thirds of your salaries in the bank every month. Like a father to a son. They agreed, and when they amassed $65,000, they went to the bank for a loan. Starting up a farm—land, stock, equipment—is an enormous investment. Two young men, still in their early twenties who had already saved that much money, impressed the bank's loan officers. They got the loan to start their businesses.

A little later in the morning, joined by Martin, they decided a few cows close to birth needed some help. A lot of the calves are born without help—a cow drops a calf during the night, in the morning there's an addition to the herd. They guide the first of two cows into an enclosed area in the corner of the corral—she's not restrained, just kept in a manageable area. The birth of a calf, I'm sorry to disappoint you, is not like in the movie *City Slickers* where the actor helps a cow give birth and triumphantly pulls it from her in a whoosh of music, and then, astonished by this miracle of birth, he adopts the calf as a pet and later flies it home to the suburb where he lives. Everything here is matter-of-fact, routine—these two men have done this together thousands and thousands of times.

Pete reaches (I mean that literally: He reaches, with both hands, into the cow's vagina) into the cow and attaches a small chain around the calf's forefeet. A calf emerges front feet, then head, first. The chain is attached to a hand crank on a metal pole. One end of this pole has a rounded brace that fits around the cow's rump and the other end fits around Pete's waist. He cranks it, the chain tightens, and the calf is pulled out and falls the three or four feet to the ground with a wet *thunk*, wide-eyed, blinking, astonished. The look on a newborn calf's face is probably the closest thing to an expression it will wear in its lifetime. The cow immediately turned to her calf and began to lick it clean. During the birth she didn't make a sound. The second cow, smaller and younger than the first, and having her first calf, howled and bellowed throughout the process.

The woman who transcribed the tape I recorded while this was happening told me her cat, who was taking a nap on her desk as she worked, jumped up, startled and disturbed, when it heard the bellows: Some kind of primal animal identification? This cow, right after dropping her calf, walked away without even looking at it. She walked in a straight line about a hundred feet, stood there with her head down for a few minutes, shaking it a little as if she were muttering to herself, and then turned around, walked back to her calf, and began licking it. The calf, even before it stood up, was reaching for, sniffing, her udders. They copiously leaked milk.

I asked Pete and Martin what could go wrong on the farm. Were coyotes a problem? No, they were useful, actually. If a calf is stillborn, they drag it into the bushes and coyotes eat it. They cleaned up placentas, blood. Dogs were a problem sometimes. The Pauma Mission Indian Reservation borders one side of the property, and sometimes their dogs pack up at night, and dogs, unlike coyotes, will attack a vulnerable cow, one giving birth for example, and kill it, or its calf. Sometimes dogs have to be shot. Rain, too much of it, could be a problem: The previously-mentioned hay fire happened because too much rain soaked the hay and led to a spontaneous combustion fire. The year before the small river, the San Luis Rey, now nearly dry, which runs right through the middle of the property (Verboom has about one hundred acres), washed out the bridge connecting both sides of the farm. What was left of the bridge stood at least twenty-five feet above the river, so this was a powerful and very destructive flash flood. To get to the other side of the farm, only fifty yards away, took an hour's drive over and around a small mountain.

The biggest problem for small (if 1,000 cows doesn't seem

small, it is nowadays; a big farm milks 5–6,000) farmers is, you guessed it, people. Urban encroachment, it's usually called, and carries with it attendant restrictions, regulations, zoning laws, and water problems. There are a lot more people in the valley now than when the Verbooms started farming here. People, at first, seem to like the idea of living in the country, near farms. That's why they leave cities in the first place: To go where there's more room, air, where there's less crime and crowds. But there are some problems, for people, three in particular, with living near a dairy farm: 1) the smell 2) the flies 3) the dust. Bucolic visions can be quickly shattered once the olfactory reality of a working dairy farm wafts over your patio, your barbecue, and your country club. I, personally, find the smell of a pig farm worse, but not by much. Nor are chicken farms a party for the nose. The smell of horse manure I find sublime, and I have, I'm not ashamed to confess, been known to loiter by the horse drawn carriages one can hire in NYC, where I live, for a ride through Central Park.

As a result of this urban encroachment, Pete Verboom has been denied the possibility of expanding his operation, which he needs to do to keep up with his rising costs. In one of his skirmishes with the Board of Supervisors of San Diego County, he was told the reason he couldn't expand his operation any more was because "Cows don't vote," meaning, of course, that people do, and people don't appreciate too many farms too near, and people vote for politicians, therefore politicians... The price of milk, because of price controls, has remained essentially the same since 1978. After a long time battling various local and state bureaucracies, he is pulling up stakes and moving his operation upstate. His property has already been sold, and it will act as a buffer zone for a waste management landfill over the next ridge from his property. Verboom is an outspoken opponent of government price controls. He feels they stifle him and other farmers who are not only good farmers but good businessmen as well. He's optimistic that the new Republican Congress might help.

Pete Verboom has some opinions on the subject. I asked him

if he considered himself an activist in this business. He said: "Very much so, because I believe that what happens to one small farmer or one individual is going to affect everybody." He spoke quietly, but not without passion, on the subject. I believe this is why he allowed me to visit his farm and interview him. He didn't need any personal publicity. I wasn't going to help him sell milk.

Later in the afternoon, I watched one of his hands, John Parker, trim the hooves of a few cows. A hydraulic mechanism sits on the back of a flatbed truck and lifts and lowers a kind of stall for the cow. The cow is led into it. It then lifts the cow and lays it on its side on the back of the truck. The four hooves then stick out for trimming. He uses blacksmith tools like the ones I remember from childhood—huge, plier-like clippers, rasps—but this man also used an ordinary electric rotary hand sander. If he found a problem with the cow's hoof, he treated it with an antiseptic and covered it with a large, red neon bandage. The cow was lowered, released, and walked more comfortably, like a grandmother after a visit to her podiatrist, back into the corral.

I also watched the milking process in one of the two milking barns. The cows know when it's time, and they head towards the barn and begin trudging in. You don't have to whistle for them, but they get a little coaxing as they approach and start entering the barn. They first crowd into an area of maybe 100x100 feet. They pack in very tightly, with little squabble. Here they get a shower—from beneath—from dozens of showerheads (for lack of the technical term) embedded in the concrete. The water pressure is strong and sprays at crazy angles from beneath and between the crowded cows. The point of this, of course, is to clean their udders. They are also hosed down a bit from the top, but a cow's hide is not subject to much cleaning; they are washed enough to eliminate most of the mud and manure that crusts their flanks and sides from lying and walking in mud and manure. They are then prodded by the dairymen's shouts, whistles, and slaps on the rump to go where they're going, where they want to go, though not in any big hurry about it: Into individual milking stalls where the machines are attached to their udders, one metal cylinder to each of the four. The milk goes directly to the holding tank, with little or no exposure to air. You never see it except in a round glass window in a joint in the hose—it's like watching a miniature front-loading washing machine—as it draws the milk from the cow. Each cow gives up three to four gallons, twice a day, 365 days a year, no holidays off. Their udders are wiped down with an agent called "teat guard" after each milking to help keep the udders bacteria-free when they go back to their corrals.

None of these cows have names. They do all have ear tags, on each ear, in different colors, for ID/accounting purposes. Farmers are not sentimental about stock animals. The Verbooms have a dog, Jake, however, who is clearly loved; a kind of square, stocky, amiable white mutt who barked at me a few times half-heartedly when I first arrived. He quickly became a pal, and he followed Pete around through most of his chores, including climbing high onto piles of hay bales. Jake's had some rough times lately. He'd been bitten on the mouth by a rattlesnake but survived that. Jake didn't look like Lassie and probably wasn't as smart (though neither was Lassie), but he was tough. He'd also recently recovered from a broken leg—he either fell off a pile of hay bales or got stepped on by a cow, Pete wasn't sure which. I saw a picture of him with a multi-colored—as if children had written/painted on it—cast on his leg.

Pete sells all the calves born on his farm and buys heifers. I asked him if he artificially inseminated. No. They did that the old fashioned way. I asked him if it was possible that he would buy back a heifer born previously on his farm. He said that was possible, probably happened often. I asked if he might ever recognize a heifer he had pulled a few years previously. Their markings are distinctive and all different. He looked at me for a second, not sure if I was kidding (I was), and said: No.

Late in the afternoon I sat with Mrs. Verboom for an hour or so in the shade behind the house. I didn't see a swimming pool, a patio; nary a chaise lounge in sight. Her first name is Lani—spelled the Hawaiian way, Pete later told me. She is a polite, serene woman, very attractive, and, like Pete, in her mid-fifties.

She and Pete grew up together, were high school sweethearts, and married at nineteen. Born and raised in L.A., she's not from farming stock but was drawn to this life. When I asked her about life on this farm, what she loved about it, she answered by saying, without a hint of self-righteousness or excess piety, that she and Pete were believers. The Rancho Community Church is very important to them, a place to worship but also a place of community, a place where a sense of family and a sense of service to others is nourished. When I told her Pete had said that one of the things he loved about their life is the time they have together alone in the mornings, she smiled shyly, possibly even blushed a little. She spoke about playing softball on the nearby reservation: "Women's softball is really big on the reservations." These days would often end with gospel music. She spoke of Pete setting up a little petting zoo for local kids, putting a few calves in a pen, of picnics and BBQs with people from the community, the reservation, the workers. She spoke of her children and grandchildren—eleven so far, all but one a girl. Even though she was happy, their relocating puts them close to her children up north, and the prospects for dairy farming seemed better there (they have not purchased a new farm yet), there was a tinge of sadness in her voice and eyes when she spoke about this place, what they'd built here, the family they raised, the community and church they would be leaving. Listening to her, I kept thinking about a passage in Ian Frazier's wonderful book, *Great Plains*. He's visiting a town in Kansas called Nicodemus. It was founded in 1877 by black homesteaders. It's now a very small, racially-mixed community. He visited on a day they were having a community celebration: Food, music, a fashion show of ladies' hats, a dance:

> And I thought, *It could have worked!* This democracy, this land of freedom and equality and pursuit of happiness—it could have worked! There was something to it, after all. It didn't have to turn into a greedy free-for-all! We didn't have to make a mess of it and the continent and ourselves! It could

have worked! It wasn't just a joke, just a blind for the machinations of money! The Robinson sisters danced; Prince sang about *doves crying* and courage and curiosity and gentleness seemed not to be rare aberrations in the world. Nicodemus, a town with reasons enough to hold a grudge, a town with plenty of reasons not to exist at all, celebrated its Founders' Day with a show of hats and a dance revue. The Robinson sisters wove between each other, three-by-three. People cheered and whistled. The rancher who had wanted to see some break dancing clapped.

A little bit later he finishes this rhapsodic passage with:

The world looked as I wanted it to. My every breath was justified. I felt not the mild warmth of irony, not the comfort of camp, not the cheer of success and a full bank account; just plain, complete joy.

Pete joined us, and they both invited me inside to look at some family pictures. Pete asked me if I knew how much milk fat there was in whole milk. I didn't, but I assumed it was a lot more than the 3½ % it is. America's obsession with low fat foods has not helped the dairy industry. There was a baseball cap with "Got Milk?" as a logo on front sitting on the washing machine— we've all seen the clever ads on TV, part of the milk industry's marketing of itself. Before I left, Pete asked me if I'd like a glass of raw milk, taken directly from the holding tank that morning. I hadn't had a glass of raw milk for probably forty years, since before I hit double-digits. Mrs. Verboom put out a dish of homemade pastries. Lord, that milk was good—ice cold, creamy, smooth.

I had spent only a day with these people, yet I came to respect and admire, even envy, them. What I had come here for was not the farm, I realized. I had no overwhelming nostalgia for my own past and wasn't trying to recapture it by coming here. That was a long time and a very different landscape ago. I was looking for a family. Not one I could be a part of (I have my own), but one that embodied an ideal, an ideal that has a lot to do with fairness, and hard, honest work, and generosity of spirit. I am always disturbed when the American Dream is described in terms of the materialistic only—the house, the two cars—and not more in terms of ideals—justice, or, say, equality. But I sensed both here, and in a wonderful balance.

San Diego County will be losing some good people soon, some good neighbors. When this farm, this family, is gone, a piece of the heart and history of this area will be gone too. The good news is that they will not be leaving California. Nor will they be leaving America. Nor, I hope, will America be leaving them.

The Red Book

Bill Johnson, the manager and head of the Chula Vista PD crime lab, has collected twenty-or-so crime scenes, each represented by a few, and sometimes only one, photograph, in what he calls "The Red Book." He has dozens of other black binders filled with crime scene photos. But The Red Book is the crème de la crème.

Bill and his colleagues arrive after the deeds are done. He's worked as a crime scene investigator and forensic specialist for twenty-five years, so this collection is a fraction of what he's experienced in his career. Some of the pictures are grisly; some are sad, some even funny, and some just nutty-tragic. Looking through The Red Book, it struck me as a montage, a musical suite, a poem cycle, describing in images the essence of a man's life work. An act of imagination is not just an act of invention, it is also the act of choosing things unimaginable from reality. The Red Book is a distillation, with a rhythm and implicit narrative, of the cruelties and foibles, the numbness, the bent passions, the selfishness, and the breathtaking violence we humans do to ourselves and/or to each other. The things these men and women who work here see, with some regularity, can tear your spine from your body.

Johnson's first passion was flying, but an ear problem kept him from a military career or commercial piloting. He considered working as a crop duster—he wanted that badly to fly. But, reminded that a crop duster eats a lot of crop dust in his life, he turned to other things: Photography and police work. Born in Luverne, Minnesota, a few miles from the South Dakota border, Bill graduated from nearby South Dakota State College. He also has two MA degrees and a BFA degree in photography. His father was a dentist, a part-time rancher, and a WWII vet who fought in the Battle of the Bulge. Bill said he never talked about it. His mother died when he was twenty-one. In college he was a crack shot (still is) and captain of the pistol team. He married his high school sweetheart, Sandy, a public school teacher. Their son, in his late twenties, is also a teacher. They moved to California in the late 60s, and Bill entered one of the country's top schools of photography, the Brooks Institute, in Santa Barbara. After a stint as a sheriff's deputy, a tip from a friend led him to a job at the Chula Vista PD as crime scene photographer. He'd had a taste of this when, as a sheriff's deputy, someone tossed him a roll of film and told him to develop it. As he stood over the pan in the darkroom and watched the image emerge, he realized it was a young man whose face was split down the middle with an ax or machete, his eyes open and leaning in opposite directions. "Kind of an abrupt introduction to forensic photography," Bill said. The boy was one of two killed while sleeping on the beach. A third boy was badly mutilated. Bill also said: "At that moment I realized I had the opportunity to make a difference."

From The Red Book: Guy with his chin on the seat of a chair, an ordinary vinyl chair, part of a cheap dinette set. The rest of his body slumps in a loose U-shape behind him, about half of it on the floor and the rest hanging by his chin from the chair seat. I should say: Hanging by what is left of his chin. The man is dead. Dead people, people shot or stabbed or battered, always lie skewed, twisted in positions the most advanced yoga master could not duplicate. A good chunk of this man's chin is missing, and in another photograph, you can see much of his throat is also gone to pulp, torn by slugs or buck-shot, at close range, from a sawed-off shotgun.

Here's the scene: One set of bad guys burst into apartment of another set of bad guys to rip off drugs and money. The invaded bad guys are all on the floor with guns aimed at their brains. The drop, as they say, was gotten on them. One of the guys on the floor, however, not happy with this arrangement, is mouthing off, not a smart thing to do when men wired on meth point guns at your head. The boss invading-bad-guy orders one of his boys to silence the excessively verbal and negative other bad guy on the floor—shut him up with the butt of a sawed-off shotgun. The boss was not yet ready to murder, or order a murder, and the boss is dead: Shotgun banging head of bad guy on floor goes off and kills boss bad guy who ordered beating. A large pile of dirty laundry rises behind his corpse.

Bill took me on a tour of the Chula Vista PD before we got to the crime lab in the basement. We ran into a couple of SWAT guys outside. A very large officer, Scott Arsenault, who looked like he could bench press one of the new Volkswagens, was working on some modifications for the SWAT team's truck. He was recently appointed as "first man in," meaning if they must make a forced entry, say, into a building where hostages are held, he goes first. Others on the team follow quickly behind, each with a particular role. Another SWAT officer, Bruce Thiesen, joined us. He's a man of average height but ripped—huge pecs and cannonball deltoids. Is it my imagination that cops are bigger, stronger, tougher than they used to be? I didn't see many around here about whom one would make donut jokes. The Chula Vista SWAT team, founded in 1972, has never fired a shot in anger, never lost a man, a hostage, or a hostage-taker. Their record is 100%. I don't know how that measures up with SWAT teams in other similar-sized cities around the country, but it doesn't take a statistical genius to figure out none are better.

We stopped in the office that handles sex crimes, child abuse and other cases: FPU, Family Protection Unit. No one was in at the moment except dozens of stuffed animals—elephants, bears, monkeys, and some ducks, reds and yellows and blues. I didn't go back to that room.

I met one of the department's captains, Ken Dyke, saw a few other officers I'd talk to in depth later, looked in on two women transcribing crime reports—cops record them now: Less time at the typewriter, more time out on the street. Then Bill took me down to his turf: The crime lab, which includes two large evidence rooms. Designed by Bill—offices, labs, and a small meeting room. It's, at first, like walking into any one of thousands of business environments in America: Computers with Post-Its on them, soft rock playing over an intercom, a phone ringing, pictures of children and graduations.

Bill's office, small and neat, is off the main hallway, at the hub of the lab. The first thing I noticed was a huge, silver lunch box. Bill, in his mid-fifties, pipe cleaner thin (his wife told me later he weighs 1¼ pounds more than he did in high school) and impeccably dressed, wouldn't need a lunchbox that big, I thought. Turns out it's an instrument called an omnichrome, which uses ultra-violet light to pick up trace fingerprints and bloodstains. On a bookshelf, The Red Book stands out from the many others in black binders. Several of Bill's non-work photographs are on the wall: Forest and mountain wilderness shots; a stark picture, taken in Death Valley, of salt plains risen into razor-sharp crags. One photograph is a close-up of paint cracking on the wall of an old barn. Each little fragment of paint curling up at its edges hanging on, still hanging on. Later, I noticed an almost-identical pattern in some shattered windshield glass—little irregular squares or rectangles, like dried mud in a dried lakebed, or the craquelure of an old painting.

The windshield glass was laid out on a table in one of the two main lab rooms. It was an experiment Nancy Vonasek-Farrar, one of the newest crime scene investigators on Bill Johnson's team, works on in her own time. The glass was smithereened by several bullets, and Nancy is trying to reconstruct it enough, so she can find the actual bullet holes, and from each one, the bullet's trajectory into the car. It looked like a giant, impossible jigsaw puzzle. Even though Nancy pieced together large chunks of it, no image of a lake or country lane began to appear. Instead, what I saw, when Nancy pointed them out to me, were three or four bullet holes. Around the edges of a hole, the shards of glass are longer and thinner, top to bottom, than all the other shards. They frame the bullet hole like the petals of a flower. Nancy, blond and slightly tan, was a pilot in the Air Force, flying huge B-130 refueling planes, before she became a crime scene analyst. She showed me around the lab. Rodriego Viesca, a latent print examiner, who I'd talk to much more later, dusted a gun for prints. I noticed something that looked like the pants pressers you see at a drycleaners. It serves a similar purpose: Hot pressing a fingerprint helps bring it up faster. Before this device, police labs used standard steam irons to do the job. Most labs have charts on the wall and so does this one: Of bullets. There are a lot of bullet types in the world, and here you see them all in rows, in lines—line after line—fat ones, thin ones, shortest to tallest, pointy and round-headed, dum-dums, and bang-bang-you're-deads. Nancy opened a cabinet, and I saw a box marked "particle and putrefaction mask." Another box was marked "thief detection powder." I thought for a moment I might be in a *Twilight Zone* joke shop. The thief detection kit contains a kind of powder, nearly invisible, that a store-owner might use, with police assistance, if he suspects a certain employee is stealing. Spread it where the thievery allegedly takes place, and, if it gets on the hands of the thief, it'll show up under a special light.

There's another evidence examination room down here too.

It's a sterile environment, so we looked in through a window. An examination table, just like at your doctor's, with a large roll of paper at its head, stands in the middle of the room. Nobody sits on this table getting their knees knocked with little rubber hammers. This room is used for major cases, cases where they might spread out a great deal of evidence, cases where they need to keep evidence absolutely uncontaminated.

The photo lab down here's not used much because crime scene pictures are now jobbed out to a carefully-selected and secure commercial developer. I guess we all wonder if someone at the Fotomat looks at the pictures from our family BBQ or old Aunt Elsie caught with her undies showing, but whoever develops crime scene photos every day gets a real eyeful of grim reality, as opposed to quotidian reality, which is often also grim reality.

Or, sometimes, something just odd. From The Red Book: A piece of processed sandwich cheese. It's an inch and a quarter long. I knew this because in the photo a small ruler lies beneath it. In many crime scene photos the crime analyst places a ruler next to a piece of evidence: To judge exactly the width of a throat's gash, the distance between three holes in the skull to match it to a three-pronged garden tool, etc. This cheese was from a sandwich belonging to a store manager. He didn't eat the sandwich, a thief who'd broken into the store did; thereby, I think it fair to say, adding insult to injury. Bill calls this case, "The Rat That Got Away." He took an impression of the teeth marks to one of the pioneers in forensic ondontology, Dr. Skip Sperber, and got an identifiable bite mark. When Sperber compared it with their prime suspect, it didn't fit. He was there, they felt confident, but didn't eat the sandwich. The guy with him, who ate the sandwich, the cops never caught, thus: "The Rat Who Got Away."

Two expert latent print examiners work in the crime lab: Rodriego Viesca, forty-six, and Marykay Hunt, in her mid-thirties. Bill, Rodriego, and Marykay can boast well over fifty years experience among them. Take-your-breath-away beautiful, blond, and blue-eyed, Marykay is a permanent member of the staff, but now works half time—she has three small children. She told me she "rolled" her youngest child when he was one month old, meaning she took his fingerprints, and that she rolls all her kids at regular intervals. I asked if that's a latent print examiner's equivalent to standing one's kid against a doorframe and marking his/her height as he/she grows. She said yes, and she does the doorframe growth-chart too.

Rodriego is a born-and-raised Chula Vistan. He pointed out his grammar school, at G and Fifth, not far from the police station. His wife is a cell scientist, a cytotechnologist, and they have two teenage daughters. I asked Rodriego, who is also a crime scene photographer and analyst, what's the hardest thing to see on the job. Like everyone else here, and every cop I've ever spoken to, he said "murdered children." On one assignment, photographing a murdered child, he saw, for a few seconds through the viewfinder, the face of his own daughter. He said the one thing that comforted him while working on cases like this were when his daughters climbed on his knees—they'd lean back against his chest, three hearts beating, and watch a movie or a TV show.

Rodriego Viesca and Bill Johnson were the primary crime scene analysts on the Jenny Rojas murder case. Most San Diegans are familiar with it—over sixty articles appeared in the *Union Tribune* alone. Jenny, 3½, was scalded to death by her aunt and uncle, with whom she was living (along with several cousins) while her mother was in drug rehab and her father in prison. She was abused, tortured with—among other things—a hair dryer, in the months prior to her death. The water in which she died was so hot that Bill Johnson told me they found her toenails and strips of skin from the bottoms of her feet in the tub, scalded from her body. The aunt and uncle, convicted of murder, are only the second married couple in the country on death row (though in separate facilities) for the same crime. Rodriego showed me a file, several inches thick. This was a written-evidence file, though it did contain innumerable sketches and diagrams. Jenny is often represented as a stick figure lying on the floor. What I didn't see were hundreds of photographs. Rodriego took dozens of measurements on the heat of the hair dryer at different settings, and at different distances from the skin, to establish she was tortured before she died. During the trial, the DA had a chair for Jenny on which he placed a picture of her, dressed for a party, wearing angel's wings. On hundreds of pages, again and again: "Victim: Jenny Rojas, Age: 3.5." Over and over again. Other phrases jumped out at me like a snake-strike: Jenny was "3' 3" tall." "Hair, pulled in patches, from the back of her neck." "Inside lower lip trauma." There's a note written by Rodriego: "I left for coroner's office to witness autopsy." Jenny's mother, out of rehab, had another baby, which she also named Jenny. Bill begins a note with: "On 7/12/95 at 22:40 hours I got a call from the CVPD dispatcher, working a dead infant report and wanted me to go to the crime scene..." The stench at the scene was overpowering, Bill said. He wished aloud at one point that he could "bottle this smell" and use it, too, as evidence at the trial. The DA investigator said: "Can you do that?" Some state money was given to Jenny's grandmother to buy a headstone for her. She never did. Private donations eventually provided one. Page after page: "Victim: Jenny Rojas, Age: 3.5."

At one point, Rodriego "rolled" me—took me upstairs to the holding cells where they fingerprint the recently arrested. This process hasn't changed much: Alleged felon's fingers held by the print examiner, pressed on an ink pad, and rolled, from left to right, on a 7.5x7.5 inch card—right hand, including whole palm print, on front of card, left hand on back. (Another example of discrimination against left-handed people!) Rodriego also explained to me how prints are taken from someone who doesn't want his prints taken. He tries psychology first, he appeals to reason, he'll be the good cop in "good cop, bad cop" by telling them he's not a cop, which is true. He'll try patience, but when these methods fail, this is what happens. Three or four cops drag a mattress into the room. The arrestee, handcuffed behind his back, and likely with his legs shackled by now, is assisted into a face-down position on the mattress. It's not too difficult to pry open even a tightly closed fist one finger at a time. Rodriego then uses an instrument called a "morgue spoon," which looks somewhat like a shoehorn. A strip of paper is fit inside, the finger is inked and slipped into the morgue spoon, which Rodriego rolls on the finger rather than rolling the finger on it. The point is: They have a right to fingerprint you, and they will. I don't know about you, but if I was feeling recalcitrant and Rodriego wanted to fingerprint me, the mere word-coupling of "morgue" and "spoon," would very quickly get me in a cooperative mood.

Marykay told me our fingerprints are crafted in the womb, fully formed, and inimitable by the fourth month of pregnancy. A fetus's tiny hands and fingers move—touch this, press that, do the amniotic aquabatics, and these actions form the three basic characteristics of fingerprints: Loops, whorls, "which look like bulls-eyes," and arches, which look like "bumps in the road." It's the variations, the differences in these characteristics that make each print unique. What makes a print are the oils and amino acids in our skin released through sweat pores at the top of the ridges. Until recent developments in DNA analysis, fingerprints were the main foolproof method in criminal identification for many decades. Although a great deal of lifting prints is still done the old-fashioned way—dusting a surface with graphite, placing a piece of tape over the area where a print is evident, peeling the tape away, then pressing the tape on a piece of card stock—there are newer technologies all of the time and ways of getting prints from difficult surfaces. Nancy recently pulled some prints from the inside of a rubber glove used in a robbery. Computers and a system called CALID, or AFIS (Automated Fingerprint ID System)—which, as the story goes, the first time it was used, nailed Richard Ramirez, the infamous "Night Stalker" murderer and rapist—have advanced fingerprint technology. Still, Marykay said, a lot of it is old-fashioned eyeball comparison, and "the longer I've been doing this, the longer it takes." This reminded me of the writer—Flaubert?—who apologized at the end of a long letter by saying he was sorry that he didn't have time to write a shorter one. The analogy may seem a stretch, but the point is: Craft, experience, skill, attention, informed and furnished instincts.

There's no way to escape our fingerprints. An oft-told story, possibly apocryphal, says John Dillinger tried to alter his via plastic surgery, a procedure that required grafting each of his fingers to his side for weeks. It didn't work, and one assumes this particular period of hiding out was not his most pleasant. I can't help wondering: Was it the woman in the red dress that fed him every meal and performed other tasks (I will leave them to your imagination) for him during his convalescence? Is this perhaps why she agreed to set him up outside the movie theater?

From The Red Book: Death by "infernal contraption," an infernal contraption being an unusual device used to commit suicide. Simply shooting oneself, jumping off a bridge, hanging, doesn't count. The boy—he looks about eighteen or nineteen—in this picture sits on a narrow bed in a corner of a dingy room. I doubt a study exists, but let me posit this: Most indoor suicides take place in rooms with orange-brown carpeting. The boy slumps to his right. He's shot dead through the heart, but there's not a drop of blood in the picture. He's shirtless, barefoot, wearing jeans. Next to the bed is a large RCA TV box. On top of the box are a radio and a hardback book called *A Dream Out of the Body*. There's also a Polaroid picture, face up, on the book. No amount of magnification I used, looking at this photo in a photo, revealed its image. On the book's cover is a picture of a shirtless, shoeless boy wearing jeans and sitting on a bed—with a vapory spirit rising from his body. On the floor by the bed: A single wrapper from a piece of Wrigley Spearmint gum, a green pack of matches, and another book, a paperback, entitled *A Perfect City*. In the forefront of the picture is a chair, across the arms of which a rifle, upside-down, is tied. The rifle points at the boy's heart. Using cord, a candle, and some brass weights, he contrived an infernal contraption. He tied the cord around the trigger and rigged it so that when he placed a lit candle beneath the cord it burned through, which dropped the weights, which pulled the trigger. The candle gave him time to pose himself like the boy on the book cover and place his heart precisely where the bullet would strike. I've heard of literature (even poetry!) changing people's lives, but it's unfortunate no one checked this young man's reading habits and reminded him about the difference between fiction and reality. It's a shame no one explained to him that when you're dead, you're dead for a long, long time.

All of the people I met in the crime lab go about their work with a quiet intensity, a scientific focus. Billy Cox, an officer with detective status and a part-time crime scene analyst, shows those traits turned up a notch or two. He speaks rapidly, keeping the lid on his emotions but unafraid of showing them. He sat across from me at a table and before him were two or three large envelopes stuffed with photographs. It's not unusual to take two or three hundred photos of a crime scene. There are three basic types. The first, called establishing photos, might be of the outside, the entrance, and places approaching a crime scene. Gives a bigger picture. Then relationship shots—a body, for example, lying next to a coffee table, can give a sense of a room's proportions, angles, some hints of what happened. Is the coffee table overturned? Finally: Close-ups. For the terrible specifics.

Billy says he is always "an advocate for the evidence—not only for those who are guilty but also for those who are innocent." He showed me a few of the photos. They were of a mutilated young woman with wounds made by a man in a black and bloody rage. As Cox spoke, I got the feeling the viciousness of the murder added just a little more fire to his mission, which, he told me, is "To help a person who didn't get any justice in life get some justice in death." He's never gotten used to going to homicide scenes, so when he gets to one, he switches into his "scientific mode" in order to do his job with the concentration it takes. This means, often, careful maneuvering over and around huge pools of blood. He said, "The movies usually leave that part out."

Billy's from a cop family—his father is retired from this same department. He's been a cop for twenty-five years, twenty-one of them here. A motorcycle accident some years ago slowed him down a bit. He's suffered a greater tragedy as well, the greatest tragedy one can face: The death of a child. About six years ago his teenage son was killed by a drunk driver while walking across the street in front of his high school. Billy speaks to DUI offenders as a member of impact panels—families trying to articulate how drunk drivers shatter lives. He said that the families of crime victims often want to know the "mechanics of death": How exactly did their loved one die, did he suffer, and so on. Some of his fellow impact panelists describe the accidents that killed or maimed their loved ones by saying how far the body was thrown, how she lived on life support for a certain number of hours. Billy recommends that victims' families not concentrate on these mechanics, and he doesn't talk about them when he speaks of his son's death. He said he just tells the DUI offenders, "What a great kid I had and what a great hole in me his death has caused."

He sat across the table with an almost military posture, his back straight and his hands clasped in front of him. He's never read the accident report on his son's death; those are the mechanics, which he, in fact, knows all too well.

Before we parted, he told me something about the murdered woman whose pictures he held in his hands. He told me she was a big fan of a certain cartoon character and had many things—pillowcases, knickknacks, etc.—displaying this character. He made sure that a lot of these images were in the pictures: They would tell us—the judge and jury—something about her, something specific, to make her life, and therefore her death, more real, more individual. No arrests, yet, in this case.

Red Book photo: Sometimes, in art, in many things, less is more. And certainly there is artistry in Bill Johnson's Red Book—not only in the composition of the individual photographs but also in the distillation of each scene, how each picture tells, with economy as well as a metaphorical expansiveness, a big story, a sad and deeply human story, which reaches well beyond the edges of the photograph. Two black and white pictures represent this case, which needs no title. Neither shows a victim. In the middle of a road is a chalk outline of a child. The child is gone. Inside the chalk outline is an upside-down skateboard. A little to the right is one sneaker with a chalk outline drawn around it. Below the sneaker is another overturned skateboard with its wheels broken off, also outlined in chalk. In the background, a pretty, young woman in a mini-skirt walks by the scene, trying not to look.

Greg Pickett is the kind of guy that drove me nuts in high school, i.e., the kid who not only understood things like algebra, physics, trigonometry, calculus, but also actually liked them! He's very tall, wears large-lens glasses, is a former San Diego beat cop, and now has found his calling by combining his two passions: Police work and computers. He spoke about and showed me examples of some of the ways computers are changing law enforcement work. He talked animatedly, with a kind of glee. I thought of one kid just dying to show another kid a new science project or something equally as thrilling.

One useful innovation includes aerial photography. The entire city of Chula Vista has been aerially photographed, and Greg pulled up a particular neighborhood on his screen. Say they get a call of a robbery in progress at a 7-Eleven on the corner of Such and Such Street. Instead of a unit driving up to the front door and a cop jumping out, gun drawn—which might lead to a shooting or a hostage situation—different patrol cars in the area check the aerial photo on their computers. They see that if one squad car approaches the store from one direction and parks behind this fence it can observe the store from the rear without being seen. Another car waits just around a corner, blocking an escape route to a nearby freeway entrance. A third car in front, but hidden by, for example, a dumpster. Sometimes, in these positions, they'll call the store and see if the perp is already gone, if anybody's hurt. Then they approach, or wait. They make their tactical decisions with more knowledge, therefore more strength, therefore with a better chance to grab the guy while minimizing danger to citizens or themselves. Say there's a bomb threat in a particular house: The officers on the scene can tell, using the aerial photos, which houses, exactly, need to be evacuated.

Greg also showed me long lists of stolen cars and then on a map on-screen, marked with dots, where they were stolen from, times of day, types of car (the kind most-favored by car thieves in Chula Vista: Toyotas—trucks, Camrys, Corollas). Looking for patterns, waiting for "a bell to go off," Greg said. This kind of info tells the cops out on the street where things are more likely, statistically, to happen. Then they do what they call "target hardening"—pay more attention at certain times to certain areas, sometimes with undercover officers, sometimes with more frequent patrols. He made it clear, however, that this is still old-fashioned police work. Picking up a huge stack of papers, he said, "A detective might take weeks to go through this. The computer can do it in minutes." Then the detectives get the distilled info.

I felt like Greg was willing to show me his computer skills all afternoon, saying things like, "Wait'll you see this, wait'll you see this!" One of his colleagues told me earlier he was related to Confederate General George E. Pickett, of Pickett's Charge at Gettysburg. He didn't resemble pictures I've seen of General Pickett, nor did he wear his hair in heavily-perfumed ringlets like the General, and when I asked if they were related, he said no, but added that his people were from the same part of the South as Pickett. Related or not, Greg Pickett, computer crime analyst, is making his own charge (though not under enfilading fire across a mile of open ground) with his computers, his own version of sabers, mini-balls, grape-shot, and resolve.

From The Red Book: A young man, early twenties, long, stringy hair, wearing a striped T-shirt, lies face-up on a floor. His arms slightly above his head—as if in mock surprise, as if singing in a charismatic church, as if someone said to him "reach for the sky" and he responded half-heartedly. The entire top of his head, from just above his eyes, is missing. So cleanly blown away that the tops of his eyeballs, the part not normally visible when one looks at another's eyes, are exposed. The raw red of wounds like these make you wish you lived in a black-and-white world. One of three or four guys hanging out getting loaded, he got into a heated discussion about suicide. "I'd take pills," one guy says. "No, that's for pussies—I'd jump off a cliff," says another. Our friend on the floor, the most macho of his crew, grabs a shotgun, props its business end against his forehead, and pulls the trigger, or, judging by the damage, both triggers of a side-by-side shotgun.

He was just playing. He didn't know it was loaded. He looks surprised. He looks as if the last words coming into his mind were: "What the…" The words due next were carried away with the top half of his brain.

Karen Drake and Al Narcario, evidence control assistants, run the tightest ship inside the tight ship that is the crime lab—they're in charge of the evidence rooms and ultimately responsible for every piece of property stored there, including large amounts of cash, drugs, and weapons. Accompanied by Officer Don Lumb, a big, oak tree of a man, on temporary light duty because of a knee injury, and a young woman intern, Sandra Murillo, I got a tour. After signing me in, Karen unlocked the door to a large room.

It was like walking into an arsenal: Rack after rack of rifles, shotguns in rows up to the ceiling, and large piles and several milk crates full of handguns. Also knives, swords, brass knuckles, bayonets, crossbows. I looked around but didn't notice any medieval siege engines. Nor a flame-thrower. The handguns were getting ready to go on a little trip. A few times a year they "purge" the accumulated handguns—drive a truckload of them to where they're melted down and turned into rebars for highway construction. At one time they dumped them in the ocean. Karen said she used to like that. It was a day in a boat, they'd go out seven miles, and toss them overboard. There is justice in turning them into rebars, I thought: What once was a weapon intended for mayhem now helps hold up the bridges and roads, which carry myself and other citizens over innumerable chasms every day.

Karen showed me an ordinary-looking lipstick tube. When she turned it, instead of a creamy red rising, there was a pointed, two-edged blade. She showed me a comb—separate the handle from the teeth and there appears a long thin blade. Officer Lumb showed me a cane. The old sword/cane, I figured. Nope: A single-shot, large-caliber-rifle-cane. Many sawed-off shotguns (in California a shotgun with a barrel less than eighteen inches or twenty-six inches overall length is illegal) were on the shelves and poking out of boxes—ugly, stumpy, bullying things. Leaning against the wall and mostly wrapped in paper: A tree branch. No one knew why it was impounded, but a consensus guess was someone bludgeoned someone else with it.

I asked Karen what was the strangest piece of evidence she'd catalogued and stored, and one thing that came to mind was a man's finger, blown off while he tried to wrestle a gun away from his wife. It had been stored in the freezer. Perhaps he's lucky his finger was the only thing he lost. Somehow, the case was settled, and Karen recently wrote the man a letter asking if he wanted the finger back. He had yet to respond, possibly because his typing skills are diminished.

Then they escorted me to the front evidence room. The first thing I noticed was a dummy lying on top of a high rack of evidence shelves. When I asked how a dummy got to be a piece of evidence, I was told it wasn't. It wears a robber's raccoon mask. It's a teaching tool. Bill uses it to create theoretical crime scenes to train budding crime analysts. Both Bill and Rodriego not only teach their younger colleagues here, but both also teach classes at local colleges. I asked Bill if he could tell if forensics just wasn't right for a student. He said yes, "The ones who are too timid and the ones who are too interested."

When we entered this evidence room an olfactory memory struck me: Marijuana. Actually, I'd gotten faint whiffs of it when I'd walked by before. Unlikely anyone is smoking it, I thought. They also "purge" the drugs stored here a few times a year. In case it even crosses a nut-burger's mind: The SWAT team, several other officers, squad cars, don't bet against a helicopter, and who knows what else, ensure that these substances get where they're going and turn into ash. All this marijuana is sealed in boxes, but there are so many of them there's no suppressing the smell. I asked if they had drug-sniffing dogs working out of this PD. They said, "Sure." I said, "I hope you never bring those dogs down here—they'd go nuts!" The dogs, in fact, never come in the station at all—they stay in the patrol cars when on duty and live at home with their cop partners when off-duty.

We walked up and down the aisles. I saw a baby stroller:

A shoplifter's trick—it has a hidden compartment. I noticed a wrapped Xmas present: False bottom, another shoplifter's trick. A large box was labeled: "Caution: bloody clothing." They showed me big freezers and refrigerators too—not for ice cream or vegetables, not for storing one's lunch.

Then Karen showed me one even deeper level of security: A walk-in vault, opened only by a palm-print scanner that responds to Karen and two others. This is where the cash and the less bulky drugs (cocaine, heroin, methamphetamine) are kept. I was allowed to peek in but not get a close look: Certainly the first, and most likely the last, chance in my life to see stacks of $100 bills!

As we left the evidence room, I lifted my arms and asked if anyone wanted to frisk me to make sure I hadn't snatched something. They all laughed: Blackstone the Magician couldn't palm a dust ball out of this place; the gold in Fort Knox would sleep more comfortably here.

From The Red Book: The Lipstick Bandit. Everyone dreams of breaking new ground, furthering their art form a little, making the next scientific discovery, the next design advancement. Fairly early in his career—in the late 70s—Bill had one of those breakthroughs. He was the first American forensic specialist (it had been done in England a few times) to prove that lip prints are as reliable an identification technique as fingerprints. Granted, most of us don't leave our lip prints in as many places as our fingerprints but sometimes, sometimes... There's one Red Book photo, in black and white, illustrating this case: A smudge on some glass. A very large—six feet six—man in full drag: Wig, makeup, dress, and blue fuzzy slippers, robs a bank. He loses one of the slippers in the parking lot during his getaway. A pretty good clue. But Bill found a better one: The bandit, while running out of the bank, bumped into the front door with his face, leaving a smudge of pink lipstick on the glass. Bill took scrapings of the lipstick, photos, and lifted the print. When the FBI showed up (the Feds always show up at bank robberies), they'd never heard of this technique. Sometime later the bank robber was busted in Washington but broke out of jail before they could make a match. Still later, he's nabbed again, and this time the lipstick print is irrevocably matched to his lips.

Bill calls (some of his Red Book scenes he's titled, others he hasn't) this case the "Cinderella Bank Robber"—because of the lost slipper. But when I inadvertently referred to it as "The Lipstick Bandit," he liked that. HBO recently called him about including it in a show on unusual crimes. He was nonplussed about this: His job was done, on this case, a long time ago.

"Down here"—that's how everyone refers to the crime lab, evidence rooms, and offices. To get a sense of where the crimes take place, the bloody, sad remnants of which end up "down here," I rode along with Sgt. David Inumerable, married and with two young teenage sons. He's thirty-eight, looks much younger, with thick, jet-black hair combed straight back. He was born and raised in Chula Vista and has worked for the PD for seventeen years. He loves the city, his hometown, knows every street. He practically rhapsodized about growing up here, the natural beauty—ocean on one side, mountains on the other—how the town's grown and changed. The crime rate in Chula Vista is declining, as it seems to be in most places nationally, and I asked Sgt. Inumerable to what he attributed this. He said, as many cops do in California with its three strikes law, that one thing is: More bad guys in jail longer. Community involvement is a big part of it too; he said: "There's a different feeling out there on the streets—let me put it this way—now people wave with five fingers more often than with one." He gave a little credit to the popular get-the-bad-guys-reality-cop shows on TV but said they don't capture the true spirit of the job: "This job is about 90% bullshit, 10% glory—but the 10% glory makes up for the bullshit." He thinks something as simple as sending cops into schools to make it clear from an early age they're not the enemy is vitally important, and works.

I asked Sgt. Inumerable if we could drive by the apartment complex where Jenny Rojas was killed. We did. Of course it didn't look like a place where a child was tortured, murdered.

A radio call came in about a fight. Glancing at his watch and noting the address, he knew what was up. School had just let out, some junior high kids were tossing rights and lefts. He drove to a corner where he thought the kids would run to when they heard the cops were coming: Sure enough, as we pulled up, three out-of-breath kids came around the corner. They wore school uniforms—ties and jackets, ties askew, white shirts flapping. Trying to keep a straight face, he gave them a little lecture on not running from the cops. While we were there, another cruiser pulled up. Sgt. Inumerable conferred with its driver, and then this officer, Tom Biondo, a friend of Sgt. Inumerable's, said: "Wait a second, I want to show you something." He got an envelope out of his patrol car. They were recent pictures of his baby daughter. He and his wife wanted a child for fourteen years, he told me. He's on the Department's SWAT team, in his late thirties and arguably the happiest man on the planet. Later, I saw him lead a mini-SWAT approach, carrying a very large weapon, into a house that had been home-invaded and still held the possibility of the armed intruder. He wasn't smiling then, but when he came out (the guy with the gun was gone) and put away the weapon, he was.

This home invasion was just across the street and a few doors down from the house of Tom Leonard, an off-duty Chula Vista PD Watch Commander. He stood at the end of his driveway with his wife, and after Sgt. Inumerable backed-up the entry into the house (during which he advised me to duck down between two squad cars—no problem!) and everything was secure, we walked across the street to say hello. Sgt. Inumerable was thinking about buying a guitar for one of his boys. Leonard's son, who had just arrived with a pal of his, is an avid guitar player. The kid gave him some advice, said he'd be glad to help.

A little later, Sgt. Inumerable told me he's being considered for a job as an investigator for the San Diego DA's office: Regular hours, weekends off, minimal danger. He seemed torn between taking the offer and staying with regular police work. Whatever he decided, he's served well this city of his birth.

Bill Johnson told me about a recurring dream. He gets a call to go to a crime scene in the middle of the night. He goes alone, and he's not familiar with where he's going. Finally, he arrives at a big old house on a hill. It's dark, cold. No cops are on the scene as usual, no cars, and no yellow barrier tape. A winding sidewalk leads him up to a back door slamming in the wind. There's a dim light on the porch. And then he notices a small river of blood coming out the door, over the stoop, and down "step by step by step." He says to himself: "This must be the place." And he goes in.

Tiny Creatures

In Bob Parks' first (and only, as far as I know) brush with the law, he was presumed a corpse. He was about eleven years old. He'd been lying face down, very still, for so long in a vacant lot next to a cemetery, that a neighbor called the cops. Turns out he was falling in love—with insects. He was observing a wasp, a hunting wasp called *Ammophila*. Parks was so absorbed in his observations that he didn't move for a long time.

About forty-five years later, I asked Bob Parks to name his favorite wasp. *Ammophila*: After all these years. Perhaps it was her (the wasp Bob was observing was a female) shape that first drew his attention: "...her abdomen looks like a pear on the end of a length of string. Nevertheless, she is graceful and svelte. Her favorite color is black with the upper half of her abdomen an orange-red, giving quite a *chic* effect." Early in her life, *Ammophila* lounges around flowers, nips a little nectar, warms in the sun. A sybaritic life, a butterfly's life.

But when motherhood calls, she turns her attention to business:

"She loosens the sting in its sheath—that, as yet, unbloodied sword, so slender and delicate, so feminine in its daintiness—and goes a-hunting." But first, she builds a nest, a tunnel leading to a chamber in the ground. Her name means "sand lover." She removes the excavated material with her mouth and puts it in two neat piles a few inches from the entrance. She is a tireless and fastidious worker, and she finishes by closing the entrance with a pebble or small clod of dirt, many of which she will first examine and then reject before she finds the perfect fit. Then, she plugs her nest's entrance with it. Then she does something only you or I and a few other creatures can do (though I don't do it very well): She uses a tool. She selects a comparatively large stone, again inspecting and rejecting many before finding the perfect one, picks it up in her mandibles, hauls it to the nest, and "uses it to hammer down the loose soil that has been placed over it." She hides the nest so well that she must carefully memorize where it is. Then she's off, hunting, for caterpillar, the young of night-flying moths, the preferred entrée. She means to take the caterpillar alive but completely immobilized. Now, this is a problem with caterpillars because the nerves in each segment are self-controlled. Each segment is like a little engine: Knock one out and the other twelve can keep the car running more or less the same. *Ammophila* has to slip her stiletto, tipped with poison, into each segment. Sometimes, she leaves a segment or two uninjected—maybe because she needs to cook up some more venom.

There's one more important task before she hauls her prey home. Though it's helpless against the wasp, it can use its jaws to inconvenience her by grabbing onto things, slowing her down. This can't be allowed. She stands astride the caterpillar's head and bites the base of its skull. She bites very carefully, applying slight pressure to the caterpillar's brain. She raises her head to study the effect: "The brain is a delicate organ, and her patient *must* not die." The *Ammophila* Sleeper Hold—brings down the big boys every time.

Next she dashes home to open the nursery door and then

back to her prey.

It was at this point in his observations that a neighbor or passerby saw young Bob Parks and thought he might be dead.

He was watching *Ammophila* drag her booty home. This is how she does it: She flips the caterpillar on its back, bites it by the throat, and drags it beneath her, not unlike a cheetah drags an antelope. When she gets it home, she pulls it headfirst into the nest and promptly lays her egg on its side. She won't lay another egg in this nursery, though she might drag in a few more paralyzed caterpillars. Depends on how hungry her baby, how big the caterpillar. But she doesn't check again for a while. She takes a few days off. Then, refreshed, it's back to egg-making and giving the needle to caterpillars.

Shall we return to the chamber? The caterpillar's jaws are now working—the head-squeezing causes only temporary narcosis—and there's a slight throbbing under its skin. In a few days, a tiny, white, legless grub emerges from the egg and, like every newborn thing, is ravenous, but, *un*like every newborn thing, it gnaws into its cradle, which is the flesh of the caterpillar. It becomes even clearer how precise the mother wasp's sting must be: Improperly or not-fully paralyzed, the caterpillar might buck or squirm (most creatures, being eaten alive, would!) and knock the baby to its doom or crush it against the walls of the nest. Just as the surgeon's knife slips sometimes so does the mother wasp's, and some opened nests show live caterpillars and dead larvae. Most of the time it works: Fresh, juicy, twenty-four-hour room service, breakfast, lunch, dinner. Luckily, as the poet Theodore Roethke said: "Great Nature has another thing to do/To you and me…" Or does it?

Bob Parks' love of small creatures led him, eventually, to macro-photography, the photographing of very small things. He's almost completely self-taught—as a photographer, as an entomologist, lepidopterist, herpetologist, etc.—and like most autodidacts is driven, proud, devoid of self-interest, but wanting attention for his work, short on money, crafty, and self-contained. Like all autodidacts, he has read prodigiously. When I asked him what he does for a living, he said: "I convey things, sometimes people." He drives a truck or van or bus. When I first met him, he was delivering flowers. More recently, he's been working as a custodian at the San Diego Museum of Natural History, not the kind of work he usually likes, but it keeps him close to some of the creatures he loves, and he's devoted to the museum, has both taught and taken occasional classes there. He owns little and spends most of his disposable income on film and better photographic equipment, most recently a new lens, which has features that will greatly improve the pictures he takes.

Bob Parks is fifty-seven years old and about six feet tall, lean, and brown of arm and face from the sun—he spends as much time as possible in the field, photographing. His pictures have appeared in several publications and at the San Diego Museum of Natural History, as well as the San Diego Art Institute. One of his photographs was recently a finalist in a national competition and was exhibited at the Smithsonian. I never saw him wearing anything—in the field, at home, out for dinner—but a denim work-shirt, jeans, boots. Outside, in the sun, he wore a hat. On a scorching summer day, we went to the field. I like saying that: We went to the field. Specifically, we went to Palomar Mountain State Park, where Bob knew we'd find some butterflies, even though it wasn't a prime time for them.

In one of our interviews he told me about "hilltopping," the phenomena that hilltops, mountains, etc. are great places to find butterflies and all sorts of other insects. He described it as a kind of dating bar for these creatures.

There was one other person with us: Bill Johnson, also a photographer and briefly a student of Parks'. As I said, Bill's also a photographer, but his subjects are often inanimate, i.e., dead. He's the manager of the Chula Vista PD Crime Lab and a forensic photographer. As his art, and for his soul, he takes splendid nature pictures and was just learning macro-photography. I have a picture of us taken at Palomar. I must say we are quite a trio. Bob, laconic, in blue, me with some binoculars around my neck and a tape recorder in my shirt pocket, and Bill, a meticulous man in everything he does, in a kind of photographer's safari suit, film canisters lined up like shotgun shells across his vest. It turns out they knew what they were doing out there. It turns out that most of what I thought I taped didn't get taped because I plugged the microphone into the earphone jack.

As soon as we got to Palomar, we walked to a small pond with a large reed bed at one end of it. Bob knew we'd find butterflies there, and we sure did. What would be a slight blur to me, less than one of those motes we sometimes see in our peripheral vision, he would spot and identify—giving both the popular and the scientific name—and some other details about it. He'd sometimes say, after he'd given a name, that he wasn't sure if he pronounced it absolutely right. If I referred to him as an entomologist or a lepidopterist, as I did above, he would always correct me, remind me that he didn't have the academic credentials to claim those professions. Ziiiiiip—an iridescent dragonfly on one flight path and the green glint of a damselfly crosses it. I ask Bob the difference. Bingo: Dragonflies, also known as darning needles, have the reputation of being dangerous. They are: To smaller insects. Dragonflies rest with wings outstretched. They're larger. The more delicate damselfly rests with wings folded. They both lay their eggs in water, which is why there were so many of them near this pond.

We took one of the trails into the forest. I noticed a sign: Plague Warning. Since I am somewhat of a lay expert (if I am to be reincarnated let it be as a professor of medieval history!) on the Black Plague, I took this to be a good omen. Still, I made a mental note to be sure not to feed any squirrels or other rodents, something I sometimes find myself doing unconsciously.

There was also a sign about rattlesnakes. This did concern me. It's not exactly an uncommon feeling: Lots of people are not nuts about snakes. I read about them. I watch that crazy Australian guy on the Nature Channel picking up the world's deadliest and most aggressive snakes and talking sweet to them. I read somewhere that we should confront our fears. Or did I hear it in a psychiatrist's office? Or did some pop psychologist say it?

That's how to get over this fear: I'll just touch a snake. Fat fucking chance! Bob told me a story of lying down for a long time once in the desert, taking photographs of a lizard, and finally, he looks to his left, and just a few feet away, "within easy striking distance," is a rattler, which was probably there all along. If that happened to me, I wouldn't need to spend years at the Maharishi Mahesh University learning how to levitate: That would lift me right off the ground. I did just about step on a copperhead when I was a kid while climbing a half-assed mountain. My homeboys still claim it as the highest vertical leap they've ever seen by a white guy. So, snakes I was hoping we wouldn't see.

We followed a trail into the forest, Bob leading the way, identifying flora as well as insects and butterflies. We came to a flat, grassy, weedy place at the bottom of a hill. It teemed with butterflies. It's practically impossible to photograph butterflies on the wing. When they're feeding at a flower or imbibing fluids, one can usually approach. Ditto mating pairs. Courting pairs, however, are too frenetic. Basking or perching butterflies are approachable but ovipositing females (a female about the business of laying eggs) are too skittish. Bob waded into the brambles carefully, slowly, one step at a time, eyeing different butterflies, planning a route, actually, to be in position to get a good shot. It's all about timing, and angles. There's a lot of frustration, perfect opportunities are few and may last only a half-second. Parks said what one needs most is patience and knowledge, from reading "about all there is to read" because we need to know "what the hell we're looking at."

Bob seemed to have a kind of butterfly Zen thing going. The butterflies seemed more…comfortable around him. I'd heard this about him, that he was kind of a Dr. Doolittle of insects. As usual, modestly and somewhat impatiently, he explained it as just experience, a sense of what will spook them and what won't. At times, butterflies would surround him, or even light on his hand or wrist. Most never came that close to, and certainly never landed on, Bill Johnson or myself. Sometimes I could follow close enough behind him to lean over or around his shoulder while he was setting up or taking shots. Bill took a beautiful picture of Bob, the lens of his camera only a few inches from a bright yellow butterfly, called a California Dogface, perched on a neon pink thistle. I'm behind him, looking very intensely, too, but, if I remember right, I was staring at a stick, thinking: That looks like a snake to me!

Later, we took a walk in a large mountain meadow. It was too dry and hot out here for butterflies. Bob told me about a fly he likes: The Robber Fly. A fierce predator, it catches its prey—other flies, butterflies, etc., it's not picky—in the air, injects it with some kind of paralyzing fluid. It then falls to the ground, and quickly, the robber fly sucks it dry. If nature had made them the size of cocker spaniels, Bob said, there would be no humans on earth, just our husks. I like to think about stuff like that.

My interest in insects is relatively recent. I'd done some bug reading in the past, but in recent years, I've read more and more. The one book I've spent more money on than any other—the definitive E. O. Wilson and Bert Holldobler text on ants—cost me eighty bucks. Worth every penny. Put a gun to my head and demand to know my second favorite insect, I have to say the ant. (I hold my favorite until the latter parts of this to increase suspense.) That would put me with a lot of people. Much work has been done on ants. Ditto bees—one of the most beautiful books I've read recently was written a little over a hundred years ago: *The Life of the Bee*, by Maurice Maeterlinck. More about bees later.

I asked Bob what his favorite ant was. He didn't like questions like this. It was as if I asked a father which of his children he loved best. His girlfriend, now wife, Dee Norton, would often help me to get answers to questions like these. She's an intrepid, mountain-climbing (she was leaving for Kilimanjaro soon) outdoorswoman, who also works at the Natural History Museum. Forced to choose, Bob said the bearded harvester ant of the genus *Pogonomyrmex*. The *Pogonomyrmex* branch of the ant family contains among the most industrious and ingenious and some of the most vicious (in human terms) ants on the planet. *Pogonomyrmex molefaciens*, not surprisingly a Texas ant, not only harvests, but also sows. Lots of creatures harvest—in the sense of gathering food. But this ant reaps what it sows. They love the seed of a plant of the *Aristina* genus: "Ant-rice." Some ant people believe they deliberately sow it—it's always close to the burrow, they clear debris and weed the area. Other ant people believe they just sort of drop the seeds there and forget them. Because no one has yet figured out how to read an ant's mind, men have spent entire careers debating these issues. Some of them even get pretty exercised over it: Wheeler (an entomologist) pooh-poohs the idea that the ants sow the seeds deliberately. Indeed, he gets somewhat wrought-up about it, which is unusual with this levelheaded and unbiased writer. One can sense his vexation when he says, "even Texas schoolboys regard the notion as a joke." I love it when academics get in this kind of catfight. And them's fighting words: Telling a professor that schoolboys laugh at their ideas. We'll never know, although I have heard that there are two scientists—one at MIT and one at Georgia Tech—who are working on devices to read the minds of ants. Their quarrel over whose method is best (and therefore most deserving of funding) has brought me much amusement and is reminiscent of Edison and Tesla's famous squawk over AC or DC current.

Another pogo is *Pogonomyrmex barbatus*, large, fierce, and powerful. This is the species used by the ancient Mexicans for torture—staking people over their nests. The pain of their bite has been oxymoronically described as "fiery and numbing." That's what a bee sting feels like too. The pain, lasting hours, travels from their bite along the limbs and settles in the groin. These big Harvesters are tough, and some of the little ones are tough too: *Solinopsis geminata*, the "Fire Ant" of tropical America, for example. This tiny red thing gets its name from its sting, not its color. As the naturalist H. W. Bates has written of them in the Amazon: "The houses are overrun with them; they dispute every fragment of food with the inhabitants, and destroy clothing for the sake of the starch. All eatables are obliged to be suspended in baskets from the rafters, and the cords well-soaked with *copuaba* balsam, which is the only means known of preventing them from climbing. They seem to attack persons out of sheer malice." As many people know, fire ants are now in the United States and a serious problem in Southeastern states. Their range now covers about 300 million acres; they cause billions of dollars of damage, and kill a half-dozen to a dozen people every year, mostly children and older people, from allergic reactions. (To put this in perspective: Toothpicks kill one to two people per year in America.) The US Department of Agriculture has a plan to control the fire ant problem: Decapitator flies. The predator-prey relationship, in these early stages anyway, is working well, "Like a lock and key," says an entomologist for the USDA. This fly is so sharp it only attacks South American fire ants—ignoring the native species and even South American fire ants of the wrong size. They "hover like helicopters" over the fire ant, dive bombing a torpedo-shaped egg into the ant's body, then buzzing off to do it again another few hundred times to other ants. The fly's egg hatches in the ant, and the larva travels up the ant's neck into its skull, where it eats the brain. While it's doing this, it releases an enzyme that weakens the ant's joints and its head falls off. The fire ants, which are neat freaks, carry off the skulls for deposit in an out of the way "bone heap." Here the larvae finish the meal in leisure, after first sending an air tube though the ant's skull. The larvae eat the brain and are protected by the skull, the brain case. Nice work if you can get it.

Bob Parks, back at the wasp's nest, was hooked. He said the cops laughed when they approached him and found out he was watching bugs. Bob told me he'd sometimes dig up a paralyzed caterpillar to see what the wasp's egg looked like. (This is about as small as things get that he photographs: Insect eggs.) He started reading everything he could get his hands on and while still only twelve or thirteen, found his way to Dr. Charles Harbison, now deceased, but then curator of entomology at the San Diego Museum of Natural History. Harbison was generous and encouraging, directed his reading, teaching him all he could. There was some turmoil in Bob's family during these years—his parents divorced—and he saw much less of his father, a Navy man, who was at both Pearl Harbor on December 7, 1941 and aboard the S.S. Missouri during the formal Japanese surrender in Tokyo Bay, September 2, 1945. Bob has three brothers and a sister.

He'd recently purchased a new 200-millimeter macro lens and was eagerly waiting to use it. It gives him double the working distance he has with his current lens, a 105-millimeter macro lens—very helpful when trying to photograph something like butterflies and humming birds, quick, nervous creatures. The reasons to prefer a little more distance, without sacrificing detail, when photographing rattlesnakes in the wild, were previously illuminated. He's always trying to upgrade his tools, selling a lens and buying the next model up, and repeat again.

I asked him why macro-photography and not micro-photography. He said most micro-photography takes place in the lab—it needs microscopic lenses, very controlled conditions. He wants to be in the field, and he wants to capture the incredible detail, the great beauty, color, and engineering in these creatures.

Looking at some of his photographs, the colors he captures are lush and intensely alive. The verdant, early-spring-in-a-river-valley green of an Emerald Tree Boa, the blazing maraschino red feathers of an *Epidendrum* orchid surrounding a buttery yellow bird-shape at the center of its bloom, an ant caressing an Arrowhead Blue caterpillar with one feeler against the lavender bud of a lupine, the upturned slender pale green legs of a poppy's stamen—each one ending in a fluffy yellow slipper, heavily powered with golden pollen. The light each one of these gives off is the light of El Dorado over a close-by hill. Bob gets a little excited (so do I) when he talks about color. Then again I've never heard anyone talk about the color in the scales of a python. He said each scale looks like an enamel bead—there are those micro-pinheads of light turning up the fire of the color from inside. He dreams a lot in bougainvillea red. He wants things not normally seen to be seen. He quoted Georgia O'Keefe: "People never really see flowers, that's why I paint them big." He later tied his impulse to take pictures with a desire to communicate with fellow human beings. He said he likes the medium of photography because "I can not only show what's in our back yards, but also show what we're destroying." He laughed after he said this and said, "I admit to being a tree hugger, and I hate what we're doing to our land and habitats."

I asked him if he had any misadventures out in the field. He didn't like talking about himself much, but he said, in the desert once, a few guys came up to him on horseback and accused him of trespassing and looking for gold. He told them what he was really doing and then they were *sure* he was looking for gold. Once, he ran into someone on a trail in the jungles of Costa Rica. The man asked him if he were taking pictures of birds. It was a particularly good place for birders. Bob said no, he was looking for termites. Lesser known, perhaps less glamorous: The jungle is a good place for a termiter too. Speaking of mites, Bob told me there's a kind that live in certain flowers from which hummingbirds like to quaff. When the mite wants to move to a new flower, it waits for the hummingbird to arrive, and when it hovers with its tongue inserted in the flower, the mite takes a running leap onto the bird's beak, scurries up its nostril, and holes up there until the bird goes to the next blossom and then it hustles down its beak again and leaps. Timing is crucial. I don't think there is photographic evidence of a mite failing to make the leap, nor do I think the audio equipment has been invented yet that would hear its tiny scream as it plummeted a distance equal to three Empire State Buildings! Perhaps they carry backup parachutes like Evel Knievel did when he tried, but failed to leap a canyon?

Bob had a lot of stories about survival tactics of all kinds of insects, flora and fauna—the incredible adaptability and specialization creatures have devised in order to survive and perpetuate the species. One of my favorites is a kind of snake whose tail looks just like its head. It's a particularly long snake. While a mouse is gauging its distance from the snake's head within the safety range, the real head is sneaking around the mouse to snatch it from the rear. I have yet to explore the psychological reasons I am engaged by that particular predatory strategy.

Everybody's got a favorite bee, right? Bob's is *Chalicadoma pluto*, the world's largest (body length up to thirty-nine millimeters, wingspan up to sixty-three millimeters) and most mysterious. Until recently only a few specimen were known. This bee boasts the world's largest bee head!: Thirteen millimeters wide, and it has jaws to rival a stag beetle.

(A stag is a large beetle collected by schoolchildren in Japan that can be purchased at post offices there. I thought beetle purchases might be a nice thing to contemplate while waiting in line at an American PO, but when I presented the idea to the Postmaster General, a postal inspector, albeit a rookie, was sent to interview me.)

The female *Chalicadoma pluto* wears a velvety black pile, with white hairs on the lower half of the head and the first abdominal segment. I can see Bob Parks getting excited about photographing one. They seem to still exist on only a few of the remote Moluccas group of islands on the eastern end of the Malay Archipelago. This would be a dream place to go to take pictures for Bob. He'd settle for just about anywhere close to the equator, though: Insect life teems.

Another great place would be the island of New Guinea. So much has not yet been seen or photographed. *Chalicodoma* is a bull of a bee and a homebuilder who contracts out a portion of the early work. They nest in association with colonies of wood-eating termites, a species of *Microerotermes*. The termites build nests made of cellulose and saliva. They're light and durable, usually attached to the branch or trunk of a forest tree. The female *Ch. pluto* burrows into the termite carton. The termites dig a horizontal entrance tunnel and a vertical main tunnel. The bees dig their large cells off of the main tunnel. The main nest tunnel is big enough for two females to pass one another (one thinks of old movies when two obese people try to squeeze by one another in, say, a train's aisle), and sometimes more than one female may share a nest. It is thought they gain, from the termites' building skills, protection for their provisions and their young from the considerable humidity of these islands. What they do for the termites and whether their apartments are rent-controlled is unknown.

Lately, Parks has been interested in butterflies. The world's smallest butterfly, a Pygmy Blue, about the size of a man's thumbnail, can be found around San Diego. It likes salt marshes and feeds primarily on a small, introduced plant from Australia. Parks has never gotten the pictures he's wanted of one of these, despite hundreds of tries. Never got one "that quite filled the frame the way I wanted. Their wings are almost metallic, hard to get the right angle for the right light to bring out the color properly." Some of the other butterflies common to the San Diego area (I'm just picking the ones with the best names) are: Fiery Skipper (good name for a race horse!), the West Coast Lady, Purplish Copper, Gorgon Copper, Hedgerow Hairstreak, Unsilvered Fritillary (could there be a better onomatopoeic word for a species of butterfly?), Bernadino Dotted-Blue.

What's the difference between a butterfly and a moth, you ask? Butterflies fly by day, are brightly colored, have (with some exceptions) clubbed antennae. Moths: Mostly by night, dull colors. Really, butterflies are just fancy moths. Some creatures just have to show off more! Butterflies have a head, thorax, and abdomen. Adult butterflies have two pair of wings, forewings and hindwings. With the wings they do more than fly. They're used in courtship, to regulate body temperatures, to avoid predators, particularly as camouflage and deception. One tropical moth's forewing tip looks exactly like the head of a snake. When we were on Palomar, Bob showed me the hindwings of two or three butterflies that had big chomp marks taken out of them. Most attacks come from the rear. If they get nipped in a hindwing or even get it torn off, the butterfly still has a chance of escape. Injured pregnant butterflies are said to speed up the birth process if they are mortally wounded so that they can accomplish their primary task before it's time to go.

Most of us are familiar enough with the life cycle of butterflies (even before there were nature shows on TV, there were nature shows about butterflies), so I can run through it here. It has four stages: The egg, which hatches into a caterpillar (larva) and wraps itself in a pupa (chrysalis) from which emerges the adult butterfly. One of Bob's hopes is to someday get the perfect photo of a butterfly's wing just as it emerges from the chrysalis, that split second when the wet wing is parting the fine threads of the chrysalis. Most butterflies live only a few weeks. Some of the California Blues only live a few days. Blues were apparently the favorite butterfly of Vladimir Nabokov, the great writer (*Lolita*) and lepidopterist A few species live six or seven months, a couple almost a year. The adult butterfly spends its time looking for mates, mating, laying eggs, feeding, and resting.

Maybe the only difference between humans and butterflies is that humans do all of the above and have to hold jobs too! There are two primary mate-finding strategies, personal ads not being an option because of a very low rate of literacy among butterflies: Patrolling and perching, both more or less self-explanatory and, ditto, familiar. I mentioned earlier "hilltopping." The males of perching species tend to particularly favor this place for meeting females. Butterflies have a "suctorial proboscis" (a straw for a nose) and can't chew solids. They drink sugar-rich fluids—nectar, sap flows, rotting fruit, bird droppings. Just-emerged butterflies, usually males of the patrolling species, gather in groups on wet sand to imbibe water rich in salts, probably for temperature regulation.

But do I sense a bit of restlessness on the part of the reader? A certain sense of anticipation? When is he going to tell us about his favorite bug? Well, it's the beetle. I know it's yours too. Hello, my name is Tom, and I can't stop reading about beetles! It is easier when we can just admit: It's the unglamorous beetle I love the most! Not the bee and its honey, not the ant and its industriousness (and its feature movies), not the butterfly and its brilliant colors. It's the beetle, for me, and, I am not ashamed to say out loud, in print, it is the dung beetle I admire most. Was it Darwin who said he thought God's favorite creature was the beetle because He made so many of them? There are 350,000 *known* types of beetles, and some people believe as many as another 150,000 unknown types. I realize not everyone is nuts about beetles. Joseph Conrad was not. He described them in one novel as "horrid little monsters, looking malevolent in death and immobility"—he was looking at an entomologist's collection. As a child, growing up on a farm, I was paid, I think, a penny apiece for Japanese beetles I picked off the corn stalks. I often roasted them to death on the lid of the barrel where we burned our trash. Though I marveled at the green of their heads and rich copper bleeding into their carapaces, they were serious pests. Their name (they were introduced from Japan in 1917) probably had something to do with my cruelty to them—WWII was the dominant recent historical reality of the 1950s. Then there's the click beetle. Catch one and flip it on its back. In about a minute, with a loud click, it would flip into the air. Most of the time it landed on its feet. If it didn't, it rested a minute and—click—it would try again. They should teach turtles this trick!

Of my dear dung beetles, let me start with one that is not a dung beetle but a kind of fake dung beetle. There's a tropical Central American beetle called *Leistotrophus versicolor*. Like a regular dung beetle, it gets to a pile of dung posthaste but not to haul away dung for a meal. Nope. It crawls on the dung pat as if it's doing dung beetle business, but what it's really there for is the flies that also come to feast on the dung. They just sit there until a fly walks into their jaws. You want to eat flies, you go where the flies go.

Lest the reader cringe at the word "feast" when applied to excrement: Dung is loaded—because most mammals only digest a fraction of what they eat—with proteins, nutrients, good bacteria, etc. Dung comes cheap. Animals do not *defend* their dung, nor does dung, like some plants and most animals, defend itself from being eaten.

Dung beetles seem to prefer the droppings of large mammals, but they have lived on earth for over 350 million years—since before the existence of large mammals. Some scientists believe they lived on dinosaur droppings, but no beetle fossil has yet been found in petrified dinosaur poop. Someone, maybe several people, are looking, you can put that in the bank, as I write this.

Want to know one of humanity's greatest benefactors? Uncle Dung Beetle. They remove dung from sight, smell, and from beneath our feet, and what they don't immediately eat, they bury, thus putting in the soil fertilizing nitrogen that otherwise would be absorbed into the atmosphere. Beetles churn up and aerate the ground, providing as much help this way as earthworms. Their larvae eat parasitic worms and maggots found in dung, thus cutting back on the spread of disease. Some dung beetles are ultra specialists. A few species live in the rump fur of tree-climbing sloths, wait for the animal to evacuate its bowels, and at that point, leap from the fur to the dung and attach themselves to it in mid-air and ride it down to the ground—therefore becoming first claimants. There's a kind of long-necked (only kidding—about the long neck!) beetle that lives only on giraffe dung. One entomologist has said that if these beetles did not exist, the whole world would look like a cattle feedlot after months of rain that then turned crusty with heat. The whole world hip-deep in dung, carrion, bones and husks. The whole world covered with a two-day-old cow-flop, crusty on the outside, loose inside. One elephant-pie, weighing about four pounds, might be covered with 6,000 beetles within minutes of hitting the ground and be gone in a matter of hours or less. They work fast. Competition is great, and insectivores, beetle-eaters, know this is a good place to find their meals. Some beetles survive this by disguise: One looks like an undigested twig.

In Australia, the indigenous beetles couldn't keep up with all the feces of cattle and sheep, and a few dozen beetle varieties from other parts of the world were introduced in the 1960s, which greatly reduced the dung, which greatly reduced the flies that feed and breed in it, which greatly reduced incidents of "The Australian Salute," the brush of a hand across the face to chase away flies. Dung beetles are the blue-collar workers of the insect world; without them, our world falls apart, or at the very least, we live life in excrement up to our clavicles.

Let me quote a paragraph on dung beetles by the superb science writer Natalie Angier that sounds almost rhapsodic, almost Whitmanesque: "Each day, dung beetles living in the cattle ranches of Texas, the plains of Africa, the deserts of India, the meadows of the Himalayas, the dense undergrowth of the Amazon—any place where dirt and dung come together—assiduously clear away millions of tons of droppings, the great bulk of it from messy mammals like cows, horses, elephants, monkeys, and humans."

I had one more question for Bob Parks. I wanted to know how those holes got in sweaters from moths when you never saw a moth in your closet or drawer. Well, the moth doesn't stick around—it lays the egg, the egg turns to larvae and eats the sweater, then it leaves. But: It might not be moths doing this after all. Might be a very common beetle called a carpet beetle. Moths often take the rap for their dirty work. Bob told me one more thing about the carpet beetle. It's a danger to entomologists: It likes to eat insect collections!

The Bridge

"How could mere toil align thy choiring strings!" Hart Crane, the great and doomed American poet, wrote that line in astonishment about Brooklyn Bridge, which he loved not only for its architectural beauty, but also because it stood, for him, as a symbol, a synthesis, of America. The choiring strings refer literally to the hundreds of miles of crosshatched cables (it's a suspension bridge), which help hold it up. By calling them "choiring" he's making them holy, but the line is grounded in the literal as well as leaping into the metaphorical: The wind through the cables, when strong enough, makes a kind of humming music. I've heard it.

The San Diego-Coronado Bay Bridge has no choiring strings. In fact, it has no strings, no cables at all. Instead it is: A long blue banner—from some angles—held out and up, almost straight, by a strong wind and sometimes showing a slacker wind in its curves. It is a one-bar—blue—rainbow arching over the bay in fog at dawn. It's a blue piece of ribbon candy hurled from a child's hand and caught as a faint blur in the frame of a badly-focused snapshot one lost Christmas morning. It's a blue streak on the backs of thirty Daddy Long Legs with their knees straightened (and their other legs lost) under the deadweight of steel and concrete. It's a ramp upwards (particularly from Coronado to San Diego) to the sky, to vapors, to—some might say—heaven. It's a slash of light blue against the bay's darker blue and partly absorbed by, partly contrasted to the blue of the sky. And below the blue of the bridge and above the blue of the bay: The long skinny legs, pale as a banker's calves above his socks. It's to the eye like a word with a soothing vowel is to the ear. From the bay's south side it's almost straight, a bolt, connecting city to town, island—pure, lean, and practical: I will get you there fast, it says, on my blue back. From Coronado it's a huge, blue hook, its curve almost as tight as either end of a paperclip. From San Diego, approaching the bridge, for a few seconds: That paperclip straightened out. A comet's tail. A low, blue flame hurled across a chasm. The bridge's color is the color of the great ether dome of your dreams. It's hardly there at all, a wisp, at dawn or in mist, or at night, its lights and the lights of its cars look like two strings of white beads beneath which there's nothing but darkness. Steel and stone. "And I have seen night lifted in thine arms." The bridge.

It's 2.23 miles (11,179 feet) long and cost nearly $50 million. This summer (1999) it will be thirty years old. Retrofitting—earthquake-proofing (does it offend nature that we presume such a thing possible?) going on now will cost between $70 and $150 million by the time it's finished. Which end of these estimates do you think will be most accurate? It has 20,000 tons of steel in it—13,000 tons of that in structural steel and the other 7,000 in reinforcing steel. That equals the weight of about 15,384½ 1995 Honda Accords. Multiply that 15,000-plus by four and that's the approximate number of Honda Accords (or other cars smaller than Accords and trucks bigger) that cross the bridge every day. It contains 94,000 cubic yards of concrete, 40,000 linear feet of concrete pilings. Add 900,000 cubic yards of dredged fill. Some of the caissons for the towers were drilled and blasted a hundred feet into the bay's bed. A lot of weight, a lot of space. A lot of space filled. It's what's known as an orthotropic structure, a word that reminded me of "orthopedic" and made me think of aching shoulder joints and hip replacements.

What it means is: It has unequal flexibility in two perpendicular directions. Which means what it's really about is great strength, apparent sparseness, and a kind of architectural cunning. It's a design originally used by German naval engineers building battle ships. The center part of the bridge is called "the box" and spans three piers (nos. 18–21), the ones over the main shipping channels. It's the third largest orthogonic box in the country. This design is a steel-saver and contributes a slender superstructure and a smooth exterior: The braces and stiffeners are inside the box and beneath the roadway in all other parts of the bridge. That's what I mean by cunning: Instead of showing off its muscles like a suspension bridge, it keeps them all hidden inside, beneath. It doesn't have huge shoulders that brag about its strength like Golden Gate or Brooklyn Bridge.

It was originally set to be painted red like the former (red is easier and cheaper to maintain), but the planners decided on blue: It's more harmonious with the surroundings. The 2,850 feet of curved steel of the box contain the longest segments of such steel in the country. The bridge's principle architect, Robert Mosher, as I suspect of many architects and engineers, had a sculptor's eye. In 1970 he was given the Most Beautiful Bridge Award—by the American Institute of Steel Construction. I suppose one could call that a possible conflict of interest, but as far as I know no one was inclined to disagree and put forth another Most Beautiful Bridge in 1970. It took about three and a half years to build and opened officially on August 3, 1969, two summers after the Summer of Love, and during the year of San Diego's bicentennial.

It's a 4.67% grade hill you climb, driving from Coronado to San Diego: This is the ramp to the sky. The side railings are concrete blocks only thirty-four inches high—to present an unobstructed view. If you hit them, they're designed to let your car ride up a few inches and then let it slide down to the road again. Cars have gone over twice. One with three drunk sailors somehow jumped onto the railing, slid along it like a skateboarder's trick, and then over into the water. Was there a moment, a second or two, when the car teetered on the railing while gravity decided which way it would fall—back to the roadway or into the bay?

So: You're driving up to the sky and to your right or left is the sky, which begins just below your window. It needs its grade and the ninety degree angle to rise high enough to create clearance for an empty aircraft carrier to pass underneath it—about 240 feet. It takes twenty-five to thirty years to paint the bridge. It's not painted from one end to another. It's painted where it most needs painting, when it needs painting. Over fifty people—men and women—work every day to maintain it and take its tolls. The bridge is always there. Always open, twenty-four hours a day, 365 days a year.

I think the first thing Michael Martin, the bridge's toll captain, said to me was: "So do I." I had just said to him: "I think the bridge is beautiful." Captain Martin and his second in command, Lieutenant Patricia Young (there are also sergeants), because at one time all highway and bridge toll workers were peace officers, carried side arms. They're no longer packing but have kept the ranking system. I heard one story, probably apocryphal, as to why they are no longer armed: An intoxicated sheriff (in his own car) stops at the tollbooth one night and refuses to pay. After some argument the toll-taker pulls his gun. So does the sheriff. Standoff. No shots fired. No one seems to know who backed down. Did the sheriff hand over the dough? Did the toll taker wave him through, for free, with the barrel of his pistol?

Captain Martin, a trim man in his late forties, looking both a little preppy and a little military, has a splendid view of the bridge from his corner office at the Glorietta Toll Plaza: Over the tops of some trees, the great blue stream of it rushes towards San Diego as if shot off the tight curve into a straightaway home. He told me his predecessor, knowing he was dying, asked him to hold a memorial service in Tidelands Park, just across from the toll plaza and with a perfect view of the bridge. He did.

Captain Martin arranged for me to meet, the next day, Robert Morbeu, the bridge's maintenance supervisor. Bob's been with CalTran for nearly thirty years, the last decade on the bridge. His crew's headquarters is located directly below Pier 4 on the San Diego side of the bridge. The massive columns rise up from the parking lot. You can get an idea of how immense they are when you stand next to one. It makes you feel smaller than those men standing in front of the giant redwoods. Parked in the yard was a Caltran truck with a 6x6-feet orange box attached to its rear end. It's called an attenuator, and it's a crash absorber—getting rear-ended is always a danger for a vehicle stopped on the bridge.

Some months ago Bob and his crew heard a thud on the roof of the shop. It was a dog that either jumped in panic after wandering onto the bridge, or was tossed out of a car over the railing. Depending on how you feel about the potential cruelty of humans, you can choose to believe the former or the latter. The dog was pretty smashed up but didn't die, and the crew kept it while it convalesced.

Bob's five eight or nine, sandy-haired, and has about him an easygoing air and a sense of calm control that one sees in men who are utterly competent in their work. You never mistake this calm for a lack of alertness or indifference. It's men and women like him without whom a good portion of America—particularly its infrastructure—would simply crumble. He knew every bolt on the bridge and exactly what to do to keep each one in the best condition, coordinating a crew of eighteen men and women to do so every day. I learned later that he was a pretty serious tournament poker (blackjack) player. No surprise. Bob set me up to ride on the Barrier Transfer Machine (colloquially known as the Zipper or even the Zamboni), to ride with one of the bridge's tow-truck drivers, and to walk the two-mile maintenance catwalk that runs below the bridge's surface.

A tunnel inside of a bridge: That's how I thought of the catwalk when I first heard about it. At one time it was proposed an enclosed, sixteen-foot tube for bicyclists and pedestrians be built onto the bridge. That plan didn't fly. Now the bridge is open to pedestrians a few times a year for walks or runs. The catwalk is never open to the public. You enter it about a quarter of a mile onto the bridge from the San Diego side—a set of stairs lead down to a door, which looks like the entrance to a basement apartment. Through another locked door, down a ladder, and you're on it. (Note to nincompoops: These are serious doors, serious locks and monitored twenty-four hours a day.) The catwalk is open-meshed steel, with handrails about bottom-rib high. Other than some crossing beams: Air and distance to the ground and then more air and more distance to the water.

Don Elms, one of the crew, who loved it up here, took me. For some reason I walked ahead of him. Maybe I didn't want to seem spooked. Maybe I just wanted to get across as fast as I could. Don handed me a hardhat, and I soon found out why: *Bong*, my head hit a pipe. I was glad it had some practical use—I knew (like a seatbelt in a plane crash) that it sure as hell wouldn't help me if I fell. In fact, I was having a mild case of acrophobia. I gripped the handrail hard for the first hundred yards or so. Later, I heard a joke about a certain bridge worker "who does a good job keeping the handrail clean"—meaning he doesn't like to let go of it on the catwalk.

For a while it's earth below, then docks, then the water. It's a different feeling over water, scarier. A few of the crew said it was for them too. It's windy up here. Sometimes very windy. If it's too windy—a call made by Bob Morbeu—nobody works up here. The bridge is built to give a little in the wind. I asked Don if he'd ever been up there when he could feel it move. "Many times," he said. I asked him if the wind was likely to pick up today. He said he didn't know.

Here and there's a porthole with blue sky in it or the white of a cloud. A ladder was lashed with rope to the railing of the catwalk. Everything up here—every tool, bucket, etc.—has to be tied down when not in use. I spotted someone walking towards us. I asked Don if we'd have to fight with big sticks like in *Robin Hood* to see who would get to pass first. Actually, there's enough room, just, for two-way traffic. All was airy, water and wind, until we hit the box, which you enter through what looks like a bulkhead door on a ship. It's dark in the box—there's a string of lights along the catwalk and a porthole here and there, but it's so large—a boxcar in a land of giants. The light was so dim that, before my eyes adjusted, I thought a bank of electrical panels were lockers for the men who work up here.

Don led the way now, and he said there was one particular

place he wanted me to see: A large porthole, reached by a ladder, outside of which was a small balcony. Don climbed the ladder and went out onto the balcony eagerly. Another ladder, on the outside, led down to the top of one of the pier caps. I was hoping he wouldn't suggest that we descend that one. He didn't. He leaned back with his arms draped over the balcony's railing, smiling like the Lord Admiral of the Ocean Seas on his flagship, making record time around the Horn: He loved this spot, one of the best views in San Diego (it looks south towards the Strand, Imperial Beach, and Mexico), and it belongs to practically no one else but him. He invited me onto the platform, but I settled for standing on the ladder and leaning out. I don't think Don was ready to leave, but we did, continuing our trek.

After the box, the descent and the turn begin, although neither, particularly the turn, seemed very noticeable to me. Back out over the open water again, perhaps I welcomed the down slope because it quickened my journey. The catwalk ends at Pier 2, and you descend a series of stairs and ladders to the ground just feet from where the bay's water laps the Coronado shore.

We saw some painters working when we were on the catwalk. They were so swathed in protective gear that I didn't recognize them back at the shop. Their names were Bob and Julian, and they were partners—painters work in crews of at least two so they can watch each other's backs, check each other's safety equipment, etc. Bob's shoes were blue. Julian's thumbs were blue. Julian was voluble; Bob knew how to get his words in edgewise. Painters are tested regularly for drug or alcohol abuse. Their blood is checked yearly for lead and their lungs monitored—a lot of times they're painting tucked up underneath in a corner of the bridge. When they work on the outside of the bridge, they stand on scaffolding that moves on a rail. Even though it's more dangerous, they prefer it outside.

I asked Julian if he ever had a fear of heights. He said no, but now he has a great respect for heights. Everything gets five coats: Red prime, pink, light blue, dark blue, and a finish. Their thumbs and their shoes, therefore, wear different colors sometimes. They take regular training and development courses—in rigging, safety issues, etc.—even though they're veteran painters.

The Zipper is not exactly a Disneyland ride, probably because it only goes 5 mph, but is essentially on a rail, and makes a deafening noise, while at the same time creating a vibration that made my whole body feel like a struck funny bone. The Zipper's been on the bridge since 1993. It moves the concrete barriers to create an extra lane coming or going—in the morning rush hour, three lanes leaving Coronado and in the evening rush hour, three lanes back to Coronado. Before the Zipper, the job was done by hand in an operation the crew called "pull 'em and plug 'em." The barriers were orange rubber stanchions that were pulled or plugged by a worker on the back of a moving vehicle. There were hundreds of these stanchions. It was a matter of pride, when plugging, to not miss any holes. Not easy. No one ever plugged a perfect game. The closest I heard anyone ever came was two or three missed "plug 'ems."

The best part about my ride on the Zipper was Jerry Browning, one of its regular drivers. Jerry's another happy man on what felt like a crew of unusual harmony. When I noticed that Beverly Sanders, a crew leader and one of the two women working on bridge maintenance (the other is Laura, a paint crew supervisor), was limping around in a walking cast, I asked her: "They made you come to work today?" She said: "They let me come to work today." Beverly has long brown hair, almost to her waist. In her ID picture pinned to her shirt, she wears it in pigtails.

Jerry always drives the front (there are two cabs) BTM because he's a friendly guy and likes to wave to people. Several people waved and smiled as they drove past us. Jerry said many were regulars, people he sees and waves to often. Jerry sat in the driver's seat with the same kind of body language that Don Elms displayed when on the high balcony—he smiled serenely while looking over his kingdom of sky and bridge and sea. The barriers have also virtually eliminated head-on collisions on the bridge. The two (each lifts and moves the 1,400-pound barrier segments six feet to create a twelve-foot lane) vehicles move forward guided by a wire in the pavement. The lifting is done by hydraulics, and there are only three or four other machines like this in the country.

On the day I rode with Jerry, we carried several cans of paint. We stopped at a manhole, and while Jerry, and a few others lowered the large containers on a rope to the painters below, I sat in the driver's seat. Previously, I rode shotgun on a small jump seat. Jerry told me not to touch anything. There were several rows of buttons and dials to the left. Citizens of San Diego, know that as of March 31, 1999, your Zipper had 2,879.4 engine hours on its odometer. (Note to taggers: Don't try the Zipper—it's got eyeballs on it at all times.) People like the Zipper: It makes more room for their cars, and they like Jerry, and Jerry—no kidding—likes them.

When we went back to the shop for lunch, I got a chance to meet other members of the crew and to listen as they talked and kidded and ate. These kinds of rooms exist in the many thousands all over America—where working people eat, or grab a cup of coffee, get their assignments for the day, catch a breather now and then. You hear lockers slamming and the bang of a hardhat on the table. As I've said, this seemed a happy crew, and even though Bob is clearly the boss, he gets his share of ribbing too. I can freely admit (I have tenure) that I would rather eat, hang around to listen and talk in a room like this, with people like these, than eat in a faculty dining room at a college, and I sure as hell would rather hear these people discuss business than sit through a meeting of English Department professors yammering about abstractions.

I met another man at lunch. He's about five ten, shaves his skull clean (even though he has a full head of hair) once a week, has a goatee to make a Viking marauder proud, is heavily tattooed (all of which he got long before tattoos were fashionable and seems somewhat chagrined now that they are), drives a big black motorcycle, has never drunk a drop of alcohol in his life, is a former merchant marine, barroom bouncer, and truck driver. You will be very happy to see this man—if you run out of gas or break down on the bridge. He's one of the tow-truck drivers who constantly loop the bridge about sixteen hours a day. They're usually on the scene a few minutes after a breakdown is reported at a tollbooth or, more frequently, seen on one of the monitors from five cameras on the bridge. His name is Gene Harrell. He's lived in Coronado (where he looks neither like the typical townie nor the typical tourist) for fifteen years, and driving a tow truck for the bridge is his dream job.

It's very dangerous to break down or run out of gas on the bridge. Both, particularly the latter, happens a lot, and most often on the uphill climb around the curve of the bridge. Other than the grade itself, nobody had any idea why. Everyone, Gene said, no matter what kind of car they're driving, says their gas gauge is broken, i.e., it's a mechanical problem and not boneheadedness. Gene said this part of the bridge is a little spooky, even for him, and was so even before he worked on it. Although Robert Frost was dead several years before the bridge was built, he could have been thinking of it, and this part of it, when he wrote the lines: "The road at the top of the rise/Seems to come to an end/And take off into the skies."

The tow-truck driver's job is to get a disabled car off the bridge as fast as possible. Traffic can get snarled quickly, and a rear-end collision could hurt or kill someone. A story I heard a few times: A newly-wed couple, on their way from the reception at the Hotel Del to their honeymoon destination, blow a tire on the bridge. They're struck from the rear. Both killed.

The tow truck pushes you off the bridge. If you're out of gas they give you a gallon. (Note to idiots: Don't fake running out of gas on the bridge in order to get a free gallon.) If you're broken down otherwise, they'll call a private tow truck. Gene says sometimes people expect him to fix their car or change a flat for them. A car with a flat is pushed off the bridge: "Possible rim damage is not as bad as possible death," said Gene. One of the other tow-truck drivers never gets out of the cab: He pulls up behind them, tells them what he's going to do over the loudspeaker, and pushes them off.

The tow-truck drivers are also often the first on the scene if someone is threatening to jump. They get a little training in how to talk to people in this situation to try to keep them from leaping before police or other emergency workers can arrive.

That the bridge, with some frequency, draws suicides and potential suicides to it is well-known. I'm not sure if the statistics would differ from those of the Golden Gate Bridge or the Brooklyn Bridge. In the same poem of Hart Crane's I've quoted already, he writes: "Out of some subway scuttle, cell or loft/A bedlamite speeds to thy parapets/Tilting there momently, shrill shirt ballooning…" About eight to ten people per year jump from the bridge. Maybe twice that many threaten to and are talked down.

One thing was clear to me: These statistics, these facts, disturb the men and women who work the bridge. Not once did I hear the kind of joking, in order to lessen death's frequent and violent presence, that one might hear among police, say, or emergency medical personnel. I know a compassionate and thoughtful doctor who routinely uses the phrase "fly signs" (with colleagues) to indicate that someone is near death. Beverly, whom I mentioned earlier, used the term "floaters." She said they preferred "floaters," and I thought she was using the term flippantly until I asked her why. She said: "So the families have something to bury." Most people are grabbed by the current and swept out to sea. And, occasionally (three times is the figure I heard most often), someone jumps and survives. One such woman broke most of the bones in her body, recovered after several months in the hospital, went back to the bridge upon release, and jumped again. She must have desired exit badly. Hitting water after a 200-foot fall is very much like hitting cement.

I heard this story a few times, from different people: An empty car is pulled over, mid-bridge, and on the railing next to it, a pair of cowboy boots. They were aligned neatly, toes pointing out, as if their occupant had been lifted from them into another world. Another story concerned the so-called "Dapper Bandit," a bank robber known for his natty attire, who was cornered on the bridge and held many cops at bay for a few hours before finally jumping. Did he hesitate so long because he was considering the damage it would do to his suit? (Note to would-be suicides: Please don't, but if you absolutely must, please do it somewhere else. Note to people who might yell, "Jump, you asshole!" to someone threatening to jump: Don't. You could and should—someone recently was—be arrested, which will delay you much longer than a traffic tie-up and will make it clear to those who know you, if they did not already suspect, that you are a heartless moron.)

Gene picked me up at 4:30 A.M. so I could ride with him on his Saturday rounds. When I stepped out onto the sidewalk, it was so dark I didn't see him, sitting on his bike, wearing a black helmet and jacket, only about twenty feet from me. I jumped on the back of his big bike, and we hit the bridge. It was freezing, and when I lifted my head and looked over Gene's shoulder, my mouth (open, I guess, in awe or semi-terror) and cheeks flapped in the wind. I'd never been on the back (or front) of a motorcycle, in pitch dark, racing over a bridge. When we hit the upgrade, I remembered Gene's earlier comment about it—that it was a kind of Bermuda Triangle of the bridge—and I felt exhilarated. When we got to the maintenance headquarters and Gene realized he's forgotten his keys (I think he forgot them on purpose so we'd have to repeat the trip), I was delighted. We rode back to Coronado, picked up the keys, and again over the bridge. By now I saw a few streaks of pink in the sky, sneaking through cracks in the clouds. I felt like a little god. This time over I even let go of Gene's jacket (with one of my hands) and tapped my helmet tighter on my head.

His Saturday shift, which he starts earlier than usual, is Gene's favorite time on the bridge: At dawn, and with much less traffic than a regular workday. He said it feels peaceful. We looped the bridge several times in a kind of figure eight, waiting for calls over the radio or to spot something ourselves. Mid-bridge, we stopped to pick up some trash. What gets picked up when is a judgment call: Is it something a driver would swerve to avoid and maybe cause an accident, or will stopping to remove it be more dangerous for the driver of the truck or someone in a car? All sorts of things fall out of cars or off trucks. Bob Morbeau told me he saw a huge sheet of plywood fly off a truck and over the railing. A toll taker, who looked remarkably like Jack Nicholson, gave me a list off the top of his head: Ceiling fans, surfboards, a box full of wine glasses. He said that once the Navy dropped some sensitive instruments on the bridge and then didn't want to admit it because they were embarrassed they'd lost them.

As Gene gathered the trash, I looked over the rail. Enormous and silent, a freighter slid beneath my feet.

Gene, too, loves his job, loves the bridge. He's planning, in fact, to get married on the bridge, pending approval. His bride will walk from one direction on the catwalk, and he will walk from the other. Then the wedding party will descend a ladder to the top of a pier cap, where the ceremony will be held. I hope I'm invited. I hope he and his fiancée screen the guest list for acrophobics.

The next day Gene drove the boat. I wanted to see the bridge from beneath. I wanted to look up to where I had been recently looking down. We set out from the marina, and when we turned the corner by the Coronado golf course and I first saw the bridge from this angle, the south, I was again stunned by the great blue banner of it, so spare and spindly-legged, seeming so effortlessly to stretch and surge across the bay. It emanates, from here, a sense of forward movement, and immovability, at the same time, and nothing, really, seems to be holding it up. The Brooklyn Bridge is the Sing Sing Prison of bridges: Massive, medieval, so many cables crossing, holding it up from above and then gigantic legs holding it up from below. Nothing (but the sky) holds up the San Diego-Coronado Bay Bridge from above. And what holds it from beneath is so slender, slim of thigh, smooth as though electrolysis could happen to stone. Gene piloted the boat ("O my Captain...") all around and beneath the bridge, slaloming between the piers, going out further to the north, right up to the lower pier caps. These need to be maintained too: They haul a big hose out on a boat to wash the birdlime away. People on the crew take turns with this assignment. It doesn't seem to be a favorite job, but as one said: "Hey, if it's a nice day, you're out in the boat…"

Gene drove the boat and Sandy sat up front near him, taking photographs. They both made fun of me when I laid down in the bow so I could look straight up when we were beneath it. The catwalk looks a long way up and is thin as a pencil. The crossing beams and stiffeners beneath the bridge offer a kind of strict geometry to balance the fluid wildness of the bridge seen from a distance. I could barely make out the sign mid-bridge with the suicide prevention hot line number. I spotted the little crow's-nest where Don Elms stood happily the day before, surveying his kingdom. It looked so high and fragile from here that I stopped, regretting not going out on the platform with him. There is a reason people have a fear of heights: If you fall from one great enough you will die! The light poles on the bridge looked the same shape and as thin as that curved pick the dentist uses but with a bulb at the end shaped like a teardrop. There were loud bangs each time a car or a truck drove over the expansion joints, though not as loud as it was when we were in the box itself. We went further north to look from a greater distance. Different again, from every angle, different and new. From here the curve is more evident and looks as if it might draw you into its huge arms, it looks as if it's saying: "Come to me, my little boat, come to me." Again, we went under the bridge. We considered tying up to one of the pier caps—the center columns have docking facilities—but the tide was low and the water choppy. We also didn't want to annoy the harbor patrol: They wouldn't know from wherever they saw us that Gene was authorized to be here. It was getting cold, so we headed back to harbor. As we rounded the golf course point again, I watched the bridge slide from view. The water was calmer now, and I stood in the boat until we docked, trying to imagine myself an explorer returning home after charting new oceans, new lands; and proud of myself that I didn't get sea sick and bequeath my lunch to the bay in the midst of my rhapsodies.

I'm not nuts about boats either, particularly on the ocean, which we sort of were on and sort of weren't. Samuel Johnson said that being on a boat was like being in jail but with a chance of drowning. I, more or less, concur with Dr. J. on that.

One life-long Coronadan said to me: "I can't tell you what we called the bridge when it was first built," and, as so often when someone says that, she immediately said: "Brown's last erection." Meaning then-Governor Pat Brown who, as legend has it, got frustrated one day waiting for the ferry to take him to the island and exclaimed: "I don't care if they don't want this bridge, we're going to build it!" A lot of long-time Coronadans still don't like that the bridge is there. It changed Coronado rather drastically by making it more accessible. It does not, however, seem likely that it will be dismantled and removed. Most people want the tolls eliminated. (Note: They have been.) Some people worry (legitimately, I think) that if the toll booths are gone, then people will hit the island coming off the downgrade at about 80 mph. If this happens some of the houses at the end of the bridge should put up crash barriers.

Let's let former Governor Brown have the last word on the politics. He was invited to the opening ceremonies on August 3, 1969 but declined to come, sending a letter with these words: "The San Diego-Coronado Bay Bridge is one I will be proud of until the day I die and I do hope that I will be able to quietly travel that bridge some early morning because I feel it is my baby." Not many people get such a beautiful baby from their last erection.

I have traveled the bridge quietly (as quiet as it can be on a motorcycle, tow truck, and the Zipper), and I didn't feel like it was my baby. I felt like it was my mother, my big, architectural mother.

The next time you drive over from San Diego to Coronado give a little salute to Captain Martin in his office. He and his people and Bob Morbeu and his people are taking care of their big blue baby, which just bore you on its slender shoulders high over the bay, safe and swift, to an island (almost) you could (almost) only get to by boat not so long ago.

Oh Ducks

"I could love a duck!" the American poet Theodore Roethke wrote hyperbolically, manically, in one of an astonishing series of longish poems usually referred to as "The Lost Son" poems. I've always liked ducks myself. For lots of reasons. First of all, it's a funny word: "Duck." "Quack" is a funny word. I read somewhere that all words with the letter "k" in them are inherently funny. This doesn't test out 100%, however. "Ku Klux Klan" would be an example. Ditto "swastika." Also, ducks are the long distance birds, the ones that fly (and they fly so high!) in giant arrowheads each spring and fall. Also, Huey, Dewey, Louie, Donald, Unca Scrooge, Daffy—ducks who forgot their pants. I left out Daisy deliberately. In duckdom (as in most bird species) it's a drake's world; they get the color. There is something about ducks' feet and ducks' bills that, frankly, fill me with joy. One of the worst things I've ever smelled: Rotten duck eggs. A duck's feces are among the most repellant I've seen: Green and white and slimy.

One of the funniest duck stories I personally witnessed: Early 70s, somebody in my crowd is flush, and we all (five or six) go to a French restaurant. One of our party, never having tasted duck l'orange, is urged to order it. When it arrives he doesn't notice the waiter lighting the cognac and, upon seeing the flames, jumps up and begins beating them out with his napkin. This is the class of people I hung around with as a youth.

I like ducks because they look a little funny, but I know they are savvy, strong, indefatigable, and make oddly plaintive noises. As a teenager I did some bird hunting but never got a shot off at a duck except once, when, in frustration, about a hundred yards out of range, I let go both barrels of my 16-gauge side-by-side. I swear that several of the ducks on the closer side of the V lifted up their tails, like Daffy or Donald might do if Elmer took a shot at them (instead of Bugs): Their way of flipping me the bird.

I wanted to know more about ducks—wild ducks, waterfowl—and I was interested in the art of taxidermy. Of all the taxidermied creatures I've looked at, I think it's the birds, and particularly waterfowl, that look the most natural or alive. You can get a close and accurate look at their colors, which are spectacular in range and hue and pattern, iridescences found nowhere else, and all contained in the miraculous and primordial invention of nature called feathers.

Very few full-time taxidermists work in the San Diego area, and probably the only one who specializes in waterfowl is Kevin Moreau, just turned forty, who lives and runs his taxidermy business, called KWest Taxidermy, about thirty miles north of San Diego. When I first talked to him on the phone, I sensed that he was passionate not only about his work but about waterfowl in general. We arranged to meet when I got to San Diego a few days later. He called back the next day to cancel. He decided against being interviewed. He said he's gotten harassing phone calls a few times. People who think he stuffs animals slaughtered by gun-crazed hunters. His first priority is providing for his family (he and his wife, Donna, have six sons between them), and his second priority is honoring the creatures he loves. His respect for these creatures goes well beyond his taxidermy work, as you will see. He didn't want phone calls, or even the possibility thereof, interfering with his work. It took some talking, but I talked him out of not talking to me.

I went to see him. Kevin Moreau is a native San Diegan, growing up in Fletcher Hills and graduating from Grossmont High. He told me he was a decent student and went to college for a few semesters, but in the classroom was either always looking out the window or wanting to: "To see what birds I could see, which birds they were, and what they were doing." His father was an art teacher, and it was from him Kevin learned a great deal of his craft—drafting abilities, drawing and painting skills, a sense of color and line. He's about five eleven and built like a bull—his chest and shoulders, solid, and his forearms and hands are massive. He was a drummer in a rock band in his youth, and it's to that he attributes his strong forearms. Maybe so, but he works still with great muscular concentration in his hands and arms. Somebody told me once that thoracic surgeons needed very strong hands and forearms—to pry open our chests for surgery. I asked a brain surgeon, who I know, about this. He said nowadays they have surgical jaws-of-life tools to do that work for them. I wasn't sure if he was telling me the facts or if there was a touch of surgeon-rivalry involved. Whatever, Moreau not only has the strong hands of a thoracic surgeon but also the delicate touch of a brain surgeon.

He and his family live in a modest ranch house in a quiet neighborhood. When you walk in the front door, however, you enter another world. What was originally meant to be a living room is now his showroom/office and is filled with many mounted ducks and other birds, some fish, and three or four stunning tableaux/dioramas (as one might see in a natural history museum) combining sculpture and taxidermy. Each creates—simultaneously—under- and above-water scenes: Lots of ducks dive and many fish leap. There's a case filled with ribbons, most of them blue: From competitions he's entered. To remind one a large family lives here as well: A huge bucket filled with shoes and sneakers. To the left is the kitchen, dominated by two large freezers, where all the birds and fish waiting to be mounted are kept. Business is pretty good—he's about six months behind with his jobs. Off the kitchen is the living room (which was probably meant to be a dining room). Some tools of his work are here: A desk in the corner where he does most of the brush (as opposed to airbrush) painting of his show decoys—more about them later. He has two other workspaces in his dusty back yard: A canvas carport structure, where he airbrushes and carves his decoys, and a small shack where he mounts birds and fish. It's a humble operation: He's not getting rich stuffing dead animals. He does it to preserve creatures he reveres, respects, and protects. He does it to earn a living. He's one of the blessed: He gets to earn his living doing something he loves.

Kevin got his start in taxidermy when he was about ten. A friend and neighbor expressed some interest in taxidermy, and that friend's father offered to pay for a correspondence course for both of them. A different book came each month. The friend lost interest quickly, but Kevin was hooked. W. B. Yeats, the great Irish bard, exhorts, table thumps, in a poem: "Irish poets, learn your trade!" That's what Kevin, the taxidermist, did. At sixteen, he got a job working for Lyons and O'Haver, the top taxidermists in the area. He stayed there a few years, left for a few years, worked for them again for a few years. A job came up as a park ranger at Santee Lakes, and he did that for six years while continuing to work at his taxidermy part-time.

This is an example of what I mean when I say he "protects" these creatures. When he started working at Santee Lakes, he noticed there were only about six wood ducks living there, he figured all from the same family. Allow me to wax rhapsodic about wood ducks for a few sentences. Whether you believe in the genius of Nature or the genius of God, you will have to agree that on the day the wood duck was invented Nature or God was on a roll, inspired, color-drunk, visionary, feeling giddily generous: "Life is going to be a mess for these humans so let's give them something to look at to take their minds off their petty, greedy selves for whole moments at a time." I can imagine God or Nature thinking like that. Oh green and white and red and red and white and orange and dots of white on brown-going-to-scarlet! When Kevin noticed the paucity of wood ducks, he got together with some like-minded people, and they began putting up nest boxes for wood ducks. They're cavity-nesters, and there weren't many places for them to nest around the relatively new (1960s) man-made Santee Lakes. Now, there are maybe 300 wood ducks living there.

We took a ride to the lakes. He was like a kid, pointing out ducks—there were several different species there, as well as some grebes. A healthy duck can live ten to fifteen years. I've often wondered if an old duck dies on the wing—flying back from the fourteenth trip to Mexico—the graybeard duck's heart stops and down he goes. An appropriate way for a duck to die. A female lays a clutch of eight to twelve eggs a year, but predators—skunks, fox, coyote, raccoon, opossum, and large mouth bass take a lot of eggs and hatchlings. Only 10–20% of duck eggs make it to duck adulthood. Kevin noticed one female looking a little distressed. She was followed by only two ducklings, still very young. He wanted to think she'd stashed a few more in the reeds, but he knew that unlikely. He had binoculars, and he kept handing them to me and pointing out different species, and several wood ducks.

Want to know another way Kevin honors these birds? He stuffs and mounts them, and this is how it works. A customer brings him a dead duck, frozen, guts and all, as soon as possible after shooting it.

It is OK for the sensitive reader to stop now, so as not to linger on the thought of shooting to death an innocent animal. For 99% of human existence, we have been hunters and gatherers, always have been, always will be. Almost all hunters are conservationists. Almost all hunters eat every scrap of meat on everything they kill. Few hunters hunt with handguns.

The night before Moreau mounts a duck he thaws it, and it sits in a Tupperware container until morning, soaking in water and a secret chemical: Joy dishwashing soap. He took a thawed and drenched pintail duck out of the water and held it up for me. He'd cleaned it earlier. All that was left was the skin, the feathers, the bill, the feet, and five bones: Wings, legs (to the first joint) and skull. He makes a shallow incision down its belly and peels the skin and feathers off the bird in one piece. He, and his family, eat all of the meat—grilled, in stews. Or in sausage or salami. Duck salami: Sounds good to me!

When he held the dripping duck up by the neck, it was one of the most sorry-looking creatures I've seen. I've seen better-looking road kill. Its neck was grossly elongated—when it's wet, it stretches; when it dries, it shortens. It was soaked, colorless, like a limp dish rag. That would change very quickly. First, Moreau wrung out the duck. (I wonder: Have the last four words ever appeared before, in that order, in an English sentence?) Then he dips it in a tub of acetone, which degreases the duck. He removes the duck from the acetone and literally turns the duck inside out while he pats and shakes it dry. Already the duck is starting to look fuller, fluffier. Then he whips out a hair dryer and finishes off most of the drying process, and the duck, though still limp and hollow, has almost all of the life of its feathers back. He's precut five pieces of wire: One for each leg, each wing, and another for the neck. He now does something that reminds me again of the work of a doctor or nurse: As if inserting an IV into the duck's middle toe's tendon, which looks a lot like the vein in the back of a human hand, he threads the wire and works it up through the foot and leg with a few inches left over in the chest cavity. Each foot, each wing. The threading of the wire through the wings is less dramatic, like getting a hypodermic through your shirt. He runs another wire through the middle of a piece of "foam bird necking," inserts it in the duck's neck, into the skull. The wires, of course, are there so the taxidermist can position the bird in any way he wants. Doing this realistically is learned the old fashioned way: By watching thousands of living birds and by studying pictures. Most are mounted to show them in flight.

The bird is looking better and better. Kevin works very fast, eyeballs everything (no measuring tools) and makes it look easy, which is why a master craftsman is called a master craftsman. I could see his muscles and tendons in his forearms and hands working hard. In fact, he's been having problems with tendonitis lately, and he wears bands at the top of his forearms that seem to lessen the pain. He showed me the inside of the bird. The skin was a creamy white, dotted with goose bumps: The feathers pressing from the outside. It was the softest skin, I swear, I've ever touched. I could see two or three pellet marks from the shotgun that took him. Boo-hoo.

Next, Kevin stuffed the bird. A great deal of taxidermy is done now with "blanks"—you buy, from a taxidermy supply house, the inner form of a creature. If you look at catalogs, these forms seem very odd. They're made for virtually every creature on earth. They're kind of a sickly yellow color and have no (or virtually no) protuberances—antlers, gills, ears, tails, etc. They look naked, impotent, bald; ghosts of the creatures they are meant to be. Kevin still does mounts the old-fashioned way: He wraps the proper amount of excelsior (wood wool) in twine, presses it here and there to form the right shape, and in it goes. Then he sews up the bird's belly, seamlessly.

The eyes. The eyes of a creature are crucial. Realistic eyes and facial expressions are very important and how a taxidermist does eyes is one area where the men are separated from the boys. Kevin likes to give his birds "attitude" and a lot of that is in the eyes. This particular pintail takes a ten-millimeter dark brown artificial eye. Many companies make just about any eyeball you might want, every creature, and they'll even make eyes to order on specifications by the taxidermist. Moreau also called the eyes "the personality" of the duck. He says he makes his pintail eyes (he shapes the eye socket) "more football shape," avoids the "long-eyed look." The pintail's eyes are fairly easy to mount. The eyes of my favorite, the wood duck, are another matter. The eye, first of all, is rimmed by a deep, but slightly diluted (maybe with a drop of gold), scarlet. Little, evenly-spaced ridges or bumps all along the rim, when struck by sunlight, create a string of red-white-red-white Christmas lights circling the duck's eye. The eye is teardrop-shaped, tilted on its side, pointy-end forward. Next, the iris is a slightly more diluted scarlet but still a rich, creamy color. Then a round asteroid belt of light green, the color of the earliest moss to appear in a springtime New England forest, dotted with black specks. It's a circular falling star, or the head of a comet eating the tail of a comet. Then, then: The black, liquid, perfect ebony pearls, its pupils. I read a very detailed description of how to mount these eyes. I won't go into it at length, but it works best with the old method of taxidermy, using the real skull rather than a blank. The copy promotes this for accuracy: "It is important to note that when skinning and cleaning the head skin that the natural eyelids are kept intact. There is no need to trim them off and doing so would cause undue stretching of the opening—leave the lids on!" There are no minutiae in this business, meaning no detail too small to pay attention to. To do the creature justice, every hair, every feather, every fleck, each subtlety has to be considered. I like looking at specialized catalogs like this—one is reminded over and over again of the power of the human imagination and the drive towards perfection, even as we know that there is no such thing as perfect when man makes it.

There was another advertisement in one of the trade catalogs I loved: Skulls Unlimited. They're the largest supplier of skulls and skeletons, and they're a leading company "in commercial preparation of bone for colleges, taxidermists, and zoos." They also provide another service. Say you've taken an animal and you want its skeleton, for whatever reason. It's gotta be clean, very clean. That could take dozens of hours by hand, scraping, boiling, fleshing with special tools. What if you have a whole moose skeleton you want cleaned of all flesh, cartilage, fat, ligaments, everything. You send it to Skulls Unlimited, and they put the subject in a box with several hundred dermestid beetles, which "assure that over-boiled or macerated specimens are a thing of the past." It's the same job the beetles do in the wild. The dermestids are the last species of beetle to arrive at a corpse in the woods (rat, squirrel, deer, human, etc.), and they polish off the gristle, etc. They're gristle eaters. On days when I believe in reincarnation, I like to think the people in this life who didn't blink, while eating sumptuously in front of starving people, come back, in their next life, as dermestid beetles.

Kevin has row upon row of little drawers filled with bird and fish eyes. He's really zeroing in on the head now. Through this whole process, the only time the duck was out of his hand was when he put it on his workbench for a few minutes to sew it up. He takes a pair of big tweezers and pokes little bits of excelsior into the duck's head through the eye socket, and then with a larger pair of homemade wooden tweezers, he inserts more into the skull and cheeks right up the duck's bill. It looks like a crane putting his beak into a duck's mouth! He's doing this very fast, putting minute bits in each side, each spot, constantly turning, gauging. He particularly favors a fuller cheek look: "I don't like my birds looking like they flew over from Ethiopia."

I keep asking him questions, which he mostly accommodates, but every once in a while, I can sense that he wishes I weren't there, so he could be lost in his duck of the day.

Next, the eyes. He puts a dab of modeling clay in the eye socket and presses the eye to it. Next the wings and feet. He puts the wings in the position he wants and pins them to a cardboard pattern (he uses the paper from manila folders). This helps spread and further dry the feathers and allows him to arrange them more carefully—as they would look in real flight/life. He does a similar thing with the feet—spreads the toes and pins them to backing. He turns the bird around in his hands, adjusting this wing, the arc of the neck, and he hangs the bird on the wall. This pintail is in about a ¾ profile, ascending. It's not done yet. More drying, more detail work, but it looks like a real duck to me, a real duck in flight, and incredibly different than the bedraggled, absurdly long-necked dishrag he started with a few hours ago. When I remarked upon how he created a sense of movement in something still, he said: "Hawks and owls have to fly—they make their living doing that—but ducks will fly just because they love to fly." This seemed not to answer my question, but I think he was implying: Look at birds long enough, do this long enough, and you *know*.

Kevin mounts fish too, most commonly large mouth bass. Nowadays a lot of fishing is catch-and-release, but you can get a mounted fish exactly like the fish you caught.

All you have to do is measure it and/or take a quick picture before releasing it. By the size, a taxidermist can estimate the weight, and companies sell blanks to the quarter of an inch of any fish you want. The company or the taxidermist simply (well, it's not so simple) paints the blank. I brought up the possibility of shoot-and-release hunting. Perhaps in the future we'll have shotgun shells filled with little laser pellets to electronically tell you if you made the shot or not. Kevin kind of liked the idea. He thought of tiny tranquilizer pellets in shotgun shells. I asked him if the duck might then break its neck falling to earth. He said, unlikely, since wounded birds almost always landed alive. Duck wakes up, flies away. I then thought: Would this mean never, *never*, any duck salami again?

Kevin prefers mounting fish the old fashioned way also, which is called skin mounting and is much more time-consuming, does take a real fish, but ends up more specific and non-generic. A trout, for example, has spectacular colors, and each fish is unique. Gerard Manley Hopkins, the great 19th-century poet and Jesuit priest, is practically orgasmic when praising the beauty of a trout: "For rose moles all in stipple upon trout that swim…" Fr. Hopkins had few outlets—his superiors didn't allow him to publish in his lifetime—but he sure could get excited about a fish (and lots of other things), for which I am deeply grateful!

One of my favorite dioramas in Kevin's show room is a large mouth bass crashing upward through the surface of the water, maw wide and about to swallow a small bluegill in midair. The bluegill's tail is attached by an invisible wire to the inside of the bass's mouth. He's a fraction of a second from being devoured. On my honor, not using any of the techniques, say, a cartoonist can use to create expression in an animal, Kevin has managed to make the little bluegill look as if his short life is passing before his eyes. Kevin's got this drama frozen, half above water and half below. Below the waterline you see a river bottom, stones, sand, weed (which he uses to suggest the river's current) even an old fishing lure treated to look as if it's been on the river bottom for a long time. In front, hiding behind a rock, is another small bluegill, sometimes called sunfish, or, where I grew up, pumpkin seeds. People never ate them, too small and bony. Only fish ate them. This small fish is placed, angled—head slightly tilted down—so its body language gives the impression it's trying not to look (and by not watching, the monster might go away) at its pal about to be gone forever. There's another fish with its head poking out from behind a log in the rear of the diorama. It looks as if it's getting ready to make a break for it in the opposite direction of the big bass. Again, I'm astonished by how Moreau has captured so much motion, so much primal eat-or-be-eaten energy, in something absolutely rigid, still. The sides and the water surface of the diorama are made of Plexiglas, but he uses another substance, a kind of casting resin, to create the effect of the water following the fish up as he breaks the surface of the water. I told Kevin I essentially understand how one can create the sense of water falling down, but how did he create this sense of water falling, or trailing, *up*? He didn't want to go into this in too much detail—secrets of the trade—but told me that it was a very slow process, very time consuming, but necessary to "make it look real." Pressed a little, he said he studied his own hand rising quickly from water. Many, many times. He also said if it's not done right, the water will look like ice and that's not acceptable.

"To make it look real." That's the nature of this kind of homage, passion, this kind of art. I asked him about hunting. He's an avid duck hunter, though he reminded me that he could only do it sixty to ninety days a year—the whole season. Maybe he hunts twenty or thirty of those days. Ducks are one of the toughest birds to hunt. First of all, it's always cold and always wet. You sit, and sometimes lie, in a blind, calling ducks who you hope spot the decoys you're hunting over and come down to take a look: This a good place to rest? Good to feed? Is that Uncle Fred? I haven't seen him in… A canvasback comes in at about 60 mph, and you better get your shot off no more than forty yards away. Nowadays all bird shot is steel, no more lead shot, because of environmental problems with lead in the water. Steel shot is not as effective. It's a pretty fair fight. Ducks are very smart. The tiniest movement they detect that's not supposed to be there, and they're gone. They know how to keep out of range but get close enough to take a good look. There are strict limits. Certain ducks are protected. The King of Ducks, the canvasback, either can't be hunted at all or, maybe, if their numbers are looking better, a hunter could take one a day during the season. They're called the King of Ducks because they are mighty fine eating. They feed exclusively on sago pondweed and sweet-water grass. Market hunting is no longer legal. In other words, hunters can't shoot wild game and then sell it to a market or restaurant. In the 19th century, when canvasbacks were plentiful, they still sold for exorbitant prices ($5.00 for two as opposed to fifty cents for two mallards) so coveted was their flesh. How a duck tastes has a great deal to do with what it eats. Lots of ducks eat mostly fish—they tend to taste a little fishy. Wild duck meat is the leanest meat you can get. Most ducks fly thousands of miles; they're like long distance runners: Great endurance, nearly zero body fat, and long muscles.

I want to take you to another angle of Kevin's love of ducks. It's taxidermy-related but requires neither a gun nor a real creature. He carves, and then paints, show decoys he then enters in competitions all over the country. These are not decoys one hunts over. They need to do everything a hunting decoy does, but the only water they enter is in a tank so that the accuracy of how they float can be judged—by being looked at from all angles, including via a mirror above the decoy on the ceiling. These decoys are art objects, requiring skills in carving, sculpture, woodworking, painting. Being really good at one of these things after a lifetime of work is hard enough but to be able to do all of them at a high level: Tip of the hat! When Kevin paints a duck, he paints a duck *on* a duck, it's a three-dimensional object.

I have a friend who's a highly successful physician, an accomplished writer. He and his wife are also internationally-known art collectors. Almost all modern and contemporary art. I love to go to his house. He has astonishing paintings and sculptures, many by the most famous artists working today, or major 20th-century artists. He has things I've seen pictures of in books. He also has things—which he's paid many thousands of dollars for—which make me want to dope-slap him and say, "What the fuck were you thinking when you bought this?" For example, he has one sculpture that consists of a basketball floating in a rectangular fish tank. (I noticed a fish tank exactly like it in Kevin's back yard. It cost $9.99.) The sculpture sits on a table. That's it, that's all. A five-minute job. A concept…regarding what? A metaphor…regarding what? My friend owned the sculpture for a few months, and the basketball started to develop a little scrim of green scum around its waterline. My friend couldn't figure out if this was supposed to be a part of the sculpture, its meaning. But he didn't like the green scum. He considered asking the artist if the scum was part of the point, but in the end he scrubbed the basketball clean with a toothbrush. Maybe he thought his action was part of the point: Man's endless task of trying to clean what occurs in the biological world but is distasteful to man, blah, blah. Give me a break! I'll bet my child's college fund that the possibility of scum on the basketball never even occurred to the artist! I imagine him looking at the check my friend gave him and thinking, sucker, sucker, sucker. I repeat: My friend is smart, knowledgeable. Go figure.

But this is what I figure: I don't trust art that just happens; I don't trust five-minute-art. I trust *made* art. Horace, the great Latin poet, said poems (which are art objects) are *made* things. There's a contemporary artist named Chuck Close who's known mostly for huge portraits of friends. Each one takes hundreds of hours of work to make and consists of hundreds of thousands of brush strokes—he works in a manner entirely his own but which seems to have some of its origins in impressionism and pointillism. He was asked at the end of an interview what he would most like to be remembered for. He said: For making paintings "by hand."

That's what Kevin Moreau will be remembered for: He "made things by hand."

This is how he makes a decorative or show decoy. He starts by showing me a decoy he'd already carved (more of this process later), a hooded merganser. The wood duck and the hooded merganser are way up there on his list of favorite ducks. "Woodies and hoodies" he calls them. There are three kinds of mergansers—the common merganser, the red-breasted merganser, and the hooded. Kevin told me that sometimes a merganser will lay a few of her eggs in a wood duck's nest, and the wood duck will hatch and raise them as her own, thus slightly increasing the chances of the merganser keeping more of her brood alive. Clever duck. The male hooded merganser has a hood, which he can make stand up to display his colors, and to look bigger, tougher. Who he's displaying them to, of course, are lady ducks. He's a little stumpy, a fish eater, and has a blue-green iridescent face that runs into the ultra-white of the back of his head just beyond his rather beady yellow eyes. Kevin already did some of the painting and all of the carving of this bird, including attaching a black walnut keel, to keep the bird upright and balanced on the water. To get him to displace just the right amount of water, he drills little holes in the keel and inserts small dollops of lead. He said it's the same principle as when a mechanic helps to align your wheels by inserting lead weights in certain places between the tire and the rim. Kevin has a large library of reference books, thousands of pictures of different waterfowl. He has several of these books open on his desk. There's not a duck he can't identify at a hundred yards away or less. There's not a duck's sound he doesn't know. He asked me: "What kind of sound does a duck make?" I said: "I'll have to think about that for a while." He said: "They don't all quack. Only about half quack—they whistle, squeal, tweet. A pintail makes a sound almost like a cricket. The widgeon whistles, the teal peeps..." He imitated most of the sounds as he continued to paint the merganser. I noticed what looked like a piece of ordinary pocket comb on his desk. That's what it was. He uses it to put the slight grooves in the wood to help bring out the vermiculation—the little parallel lines throughout so much of a duck's plumage. At one point he uses a brush so tiny it has only a few bristles. I told him I'd read about a man who painted incredibly tiny objects and sometimes used a brush with only one bristle, *and* he would make the brushstrokes in between his own heartbeats. Kevin's work was almost as delicate: "I hold my breath on each stroke." He also uses magnifying goggles. The basketball/fish tank sculptor I mentioned earlier probably was wearing goggles, too, when he conceptualized his "sculpture": Beer goggles.

It's hard to describe the array and subtleties of the colors, the shadings, the sense of light where it's called for (the duck is painted as if in daytime under sun) the thousands of strokes and re-strokes, the palimpsests, the do-overs. As in mounting a duck, he does all this holding the duck in his left hand and painting with his right. Constantly moving it, eyeballing for symmetry. I said I thought most people did this kind of painting with the duck in a vise or fixed to something. He said: "Some guys do it that way." Meaning most guys, meaning not him. The final stage in the decoy painting is airbrushing. Even though 98% of the duck is hand-painted, the airbrush painting is crucial: It creates a softness to the duck's feathers that's much harder to get with a brush, and this softness brings out the detail. "To make wood look soft is the challenge."

A little later, Kevin showed me the earlier stages of making competition decoys. He starts with a solid block of basswood (or, sometimes, tupelo). He cuts a rough shape with a band saw, working fast (in fact, pushing the wood hard and straining the blade) and that acrid, sharp smell of friction-scorched wood rises into the air. After he gets the rough shape, he sits at the bench, and using a sander with a large round-headed carbide bit, he brings the duck out of the wood. As usual: Duck in one hand, tool in another. He said, "I can see the duck in the wood." He didn't know that Michelangelo said a similar thing about the figure being inside the block, and all he had to do was remove the marble around it. Within an hour, hour-and-a-half, he had a pretty smooth, but still not close to being painted, merganser.

I looked down after Kevin had been sanding for quite a while and noticed that his big, friendly black Lab retriever was lying under the blizzard of sawdust. He was almost completely covered but unfazed. His name is Zephyr. Kevin said only two things get him excited: In a bad way if a bug lands on him and in a good way when he sees Kevin take one of his shotguns from the rack and Zephyr knows he's going hunting, which he was born to do.

What do we call Moreau? A painter, a taxidermist, a sculptor, a carver? All of those. I'd call him an artist and—I've put my eyeballs on his work—a damn good one.

I wanted to talk to him a little bit more about hunting. As I said, I hunted as a teenager and although not good at it, I liked tramping around in the woods. I'd recently moved to Georgia and bought a few long guns: A Winchester 30-30 carbine (the rifle the cowboys carry in the movies) and a 20-gauge side-by-side double barrel. The few times I shot the rifle it made too much noise. I did shoot a baseball with it to see what happens. Answer: It blows a big hole in it. But the 30-30's gonna stay on the rack. I've taken up skeet shooting and am thinking it might be the sport of my dotage. I might try some bird hunting, pheasant, maybe, or quail. I don't think I want to hunt ducks. It's too cold and wet, and you have to get up too early.

I asked Kevin how often he hunted. Anything else but ducks? He went as often as possible during the sixty- to ninety-day season and hardly ever hunted anything else. He didn't have any macho hunting stories. Instead, he wanted to tell me about a solo duck-hunting trip he took to the Salton Sea, the primary duck hunting area in Southern California. The Salton Sea is about seventy-five miles northeast of San Diego and is less than a hundred years old—it was formed when the Colorado River knocked out irrigation dikes and flooded a part of the desert called the Salt Sink. It's in trouble now, drying up, and getting saltier. It's already about 25% saltier than the Pacific Ocean. Studies have shown, however, that the water meets federal standards for drinking. This sounds a little odd to me since it's 25% saltier than the Pacific, and we don't drink the Pacific. But, I got this news from the *New York Times*, and as we all know, The Gray Lady never gets it wrong.

The Salton Sea is a major stopover and wintering place along the Pacific Flyway, which 15–30 million birds travel each year. If the Salton dies, there will be big time problems for migrating waterfowl.

Kevin got to the sea in the middle of the night and slept for a few hours in the back of his truck. He was up about 4:30. He'd planned to hunt from a rowboat, but the water was too choppy, spray blowing off the top of the waves: Spindrift. There was a full moon, and it hung just over the sea and was "the biggest I've ever seen." Instead of the boat, Kevin walked out on a long rock jetty. He was awestruck and a little sad that he was experiencing this alone. The wind, the water, the moonlight, and walking out on the rocks made him feel he was becoming more a part of the landscape, made him understand how small we humans are next to the grandeur of Nature, or God. He was thrilled, he felt blessed to be a part of this. He told me this story a few times, each time his eyes lighting with the memory, each time struggling to find the words to describe what he felt—it was spiritual, epiphanic, deeply moving. Later, he wrote one of the two poems he has written in his life. The other was a love poem to his wife. He recited the poem to me from memory. Here are a few lines: "So I turned and faced the restless wind./It took more strength to stand therein/ but the effort was worth the magnificent sight./Stars danced and played on troubled seas/I felt so alone but privileged to be…" It is unlikely that Kevin will be among the American poets after his death, but honestly, just as I'd much prefer to look at one of his ducks—either mounted or painted—than look at the basketball in the fish tank, I found more pleasure in his poem than in the literary equivalent (oh there are many, tedious and pretentious, beyond imagining) of the basketball/fish tank.

I had asked him for a hunting story but didn't get it. I don't know if he even saw a duck that day, let alone took one. About the only specific hunting comment I found in all my notes and tapes of our time together was: "The canvasbacks, they come in like F-14s and will make a fool out of a hunter."

On our last day together I told him I knew something about ducks that I bet he didn't know. He gave me an "Oh, yeah?" look. I told him a duck's quack doesn't echo.* Sound technicians, audio experts, scientists, etc., have no idea why this is true. Tests are ongoing. He *didn't* know that. Somehow that had never come up in his work.

Here's his recipe for BBQ'd duck: Cut duck meat into about one-inch squares. Marinate in Italian salad dressing for a few hours. Wrap each piece in a half piece of bacon (duck meat, as mentioned, is very lean and will dry out quickly). Cook it fast over a hot fire. Cook only long enough that the "bacon looks edible." I tried it: Tasty, tasty, tasty. I had to use store-bought duck. But someday, someday, somewhere, there will be canvasback for me.

*This turned out not to be true.

Eat Fire

One thing I've learned: Go looking for fire-eaters, and you don't know what you'll find. After putting out the word (I have a few, um, unique friends in the San Diego area) that I was looking for fire-eaters, after internet searches, after placing an ad in a newspaper, I found two fire-eaters in San Diego and got several more leads on fire-eaters in Tijuana. Actually, I found one fire-eater in San Diego, and she was willing not only to demonstrate her craft to me but also willing to teach someone else, initiate another, into the society of fire-eaters. Therein lies a good deal of this tale.

Let me tell you something about the initiate first. JunkBoy is his name, and I'll hereafter refer to him as JB. It doesn't say "JunkBoy" on his birth certificate. It's his stage name, his nom de plume, and his alter ego. He's a born and bred San Diegan, about five feet ten, has medium-length sandy hair, wears one of those tiny beards just below the middle of his lower lip, and looks younger than his thirty-eight years—and this is a man whose body, as you will see, has taken more than the usual wear and tear.

One of the first things JB said when we met was: "I strap large amounts of explosives to my body and blow myself up." Trying to act nonchalant, I scanned the room for the nearest exit. Given what's going on in the world, this did not strike me as a good act for your average cabaret. I want to make it clear he hasn't done this publicly since before 9/11. JB (judge for yourself) may be a little crazy, but he's not dumb. A machinist by trade, he's made himself a steel chest protector. Very importantly, JB has access to professional pyrotechnic materials supplied to him by a man known as PyroBoy (natch). You could never get PyroBoy's real name from JB, even if you used grisly torture. (Whereas, you could get from me JB's real name if you worked me over with a hose made of whipped cream.) As you will see, he is almost impervious to pain.

This is what he does: He hot-glues four or five rows of brick firecrackers to a black powder tape called "quickmatch," which he then glues to the breastplate. Then he adds several "gerbs"—devices that shoot out sparks. Then some percussion devices: "Not so much explosives as noisemakers." Next, he attaches all this to a 9-volt igniter box "with a safety switch." He puts a sheet of Mylar under the breastplate and puts a shirt on over it all. He says it's a little bulky, but if he wears a coat it's hardly noticeable. He plans a route to and from the place of his "performance," always the kind of club where edgy acts take place, climbs on the stage unannounced, behaves boorishly until he starts getting heckled, and then he hits the switch.

The explosion is designed to take place right on his chest with very little outward or upward thrust. He makes sure he's several feet from the first row. Sometimes, he says, paper from the crackers and even a loose cracker or two, reaches the audience, but nobody, including himself, has ever been hurt. Though, he says: "My shirt usually catches fire." He runs out and disappears a few seconds after the explosion.

I am one of those people, employed by a university English department, who still believes language is not The Betrayer, that, though not perfect, it is still by far the best way we have of communicating with each other. So I asked him what he called what he did. "Gosh, performance art, shock art, hit and run art." I thought to call it Rubber Neck Art: Like a car crash—we may not want to look but we must. I remembered the performance artist who covered her body with slices of baloney—a euphemism for her talent? Most performance art I've seen over the years struck me as banal and pretentious, and usually with a PC point as subtle as an ice pick in the eyeball. It always whiffed of narcissism, an excuse to climb on stage, preferably alone. It always seemed to me to lack discipline, a true passion to make something. Why study dance or singing or even writing when you can jump on a stage, act self-indulgently and call it art?

But there was something very different about JB and his motives. Namely, he doesn't seem to have any, at least not conscious, motives. After blowing up, he doesn't hang around waiting for applause. And, as you will see, there is nothing self-flattering about any of the other feats he performs. He is aware of the extreme commercial limitations in what he does. Indeed: He is much more at risk of being fined than getting paid for his work. "I do it (remember he is referring to not only exploding but also other feats as yet unspecified) for the reaction, that's what I kind of get off on."

He loved horror movies as a child and dressed up as characters to scare the other kids, unconfined by Halloween. He became obsessed with Houdini and read voraciously about him. One thing he never forgot about Houdini: Much of his early career was spent hanging around with freaks and other sideshow people. JB knows the movie *Freaks* almost frame by frame. He taught himself many escape acts. He loved magic and was good at sleight of hand but "always too fast."

If you're wondering about his childhood: Pretty normal. His

parents were divorced when he was a young teenager, but he's close to both of them and a brother, and he visits his Grammy regularly. He had a monkey for twenty-seven years, recently deceased, whom he mourns. The monkey was fed LSD by previous owners and therefore was a little jumpy. She (her name was Onion) had a lifelong fear of brooms and gloves. One can only shudder thinking of what those heinous hippies did to bum out the poor monkey in such a way. JB had some bad boy years and his share of run-ins with booze and drugs, but he's been clean and sober for some time now and in a stable relationship.

OK: What else does JB do? When he is not exploding, of what does his act consist? He inhales condoms through his nose and pulls them out his mouth. This was the first feat of his career, and it began on a bet from a former girlfriend: "Twenty bucks says you can't inhale that condom." He did it first try. What kind does he use? "Ribbed, for my pleasure," he says, and "unlubricated because the spermicide tastes lousy." He eats king worms and crickets. Sometimes he'll chew a mouthful of crickets and, feeling a few still alive in one cheek, will then open his mouth and let the living cricket or two crawl over their dead and half-masticated comrades to his lips and onto his chin and freedom. These he later releases into the wild. Ours is not to reason why. But I asked: "What's up with the worm and bug eating?" JB, nonplussed: "I'm a big fan of protein, there's a lot of protein in bugs and worms." I assumed crickets are pretty crunchy. "Yeah, they're a little crunchy, and they've got a strange bitter taste. So do king worms—really bitter. Must be a defense mechanism, like ants when you crush them, they smell funny." Uh-huh. He's searching for maggots but can't find any commercially, and it's too difficult to gather enough from the festering wounds of road kill. He'd put this little twist on maggot eating (as if maggot eating wasn't twisted enough): "Everybody has this thing about maggots looking like rice." I thought: Sure, every time someone mentioned white rice someone else would bring up maggots. "I'd bring 'em in a Chinese food carton and just start spooning them up." I guess he is one of those people, like myself, who are clumsy with chopsticks. He talks about eating maggots in the same way other people talk about going out to the front porch to pick up the newspaper.

What else? He puts a four-inch electrical drill up his nose and turns it on, or inserts it while it's already turned on. He pounds a spike into his nose with a hammer and then pulls it out with the claw end. He swallows butane gas, swallows several puffs of cigarette smoke, waits until he feels a burp coming up, dips his hand in dishwashing liquid, makes an O with his thumb and forefinger, burps a bubble of butane gas and smoke into this O and, while the bubble is still stuck to his hand, lights it: Boom! It "makes a little mushroom cloud of smoke just like an atomic blast." I asked him if he ever consulted his internist about the long-term effects of swallowing butane gas, and he said, "I figure if I'm burping it right up, it can't do me any harm." This guy is crackers. I love this guy.

JB wanted desperately to learn how to eat fire. He also wanted to learn to sword swallow but was procrastinating: "People can get killed doing that." But he wanted to learn to eat fire, and I could help him.

In fact, I had the perfect teacher for him, an experienced fire-eater with a pedagogical bent. Her name is Karen Shelby; she's thirty-one years old, a Ph.D. student at UC San Diego. Her field is Political Science with a special interest in women in politics. She's writing her dissertation on Simone de Beauvoir and women and the Algerian War. Beauvoir was a French proto-feminist who wrote the seminal book, *The Second Sex*. She was a lover of, among others, the French existentialist Jean Paul Sartre. Brilliant, immensely gifted, independent, she always reminded me of Lou Andreas Salome, a woman about two generations older, and a lover of both Rilke (the poet) and Nietzsche (the philosopher), and protégé of Freud (the shrink). She told Rilke to eat rocks (he was a whiner) and found Nietzsche breathtakingly neurasthenic and needing a whip. What I love most about her, though, is that when she was old and knew she was dying, she was pissed off. Not afraid, sad, etc. Pissed off. She had too much more to do.

Karen will be a professor in a few years and is married to a young professor of linguistics. Karen did her undergraduate work at the University of Louisville in Kentucky and learned to eat fire from a woman named Liz Carter, the wife of a University of Louisville dean. Carter asked (it was an outdoor gathering) if anyone wanted to learn to eat fire—not your usual invitation at a student/faculty picnic. Karen and a few others stepped forward. The others backed off when the reality of putting a flaming torch in their mouths and closing their lips and teeth around it, sunk in. Karen's an attractive brunette, very articulate, and one of the most naturally and continuously ebullient people I have ever met. Ten minutes around her could pull the darkest person out of the deepest funk.

I met Karen and talked to her before she gave me a demonstration. I was struck by her normalcy, particularly compared to JB.

I asked Karen if she was an eccentric child. "No, I was a smart kid, got good grades…but I did follow my own mind." She has no ambitions to further her fire-eating career—she only does it a handful of times per year, usually at a party or picnic. Her parents (divorced since she, too, was a young teenager and, respectively, a mortgage banker and a lawyer) are blasé about it, but her husband, Eric, loves it. In fact, they met and fell in love over fire-eating. While graduate students at Rutgers, they were both at a baby shower when they met. She was beaming. He approached her and asked what she was smiling so broadly about. Not a bad opening line—it's simple, plausible, original enough, and made it clear he was attracted first to an element of Karen's personality rather than just her looks. Karen responded: "I just ate fire." Even better answer. He was fascinated, impressed, and BAM, just like that, he was a goner. I asked her if he still liked that she eats fire. She said: "Oh he's very excited when I'm going to eat fire!"

I got a close-up demonstration of fire-eating in the kitchen of my rented condo in Coronado. I was a little nervous about this. The woman next door had, obviously, been elected (by a landslide!) to the office of Village Scold and took her responsibilities seriously.

There's a note on the refrigerator of the condo that says, "No laughing or dish washing after ten o'clock." She'd left a note once saying I opened and closed my door too often.

I pulled the shades. "The kitchen floor is tiled and the ceilings high," Karen said, and "I like the proximity to water."

There is one basic spoken but unwritten rule about fire-eating: You don't reveal its secrets unless you pass them along, teaching another to eat fire. You can explain technique, but the real secret to eating fire is not technique—that can be pretty much figured out by close observation. The secret is in the sauce, the flammable liquid, the torches are dipped into before they're lit. Karen calls it, appropriately, "secret sauce," and never revealed to me what it was. I had considered trying to learn to eat fire myself, but after I met JB and figured out 1) He's nuts and 2) He very much wanted to learn, I decided: Better him than me. I'd be the enabler.

First, Karen showed me her tools, including a jar of the secret sauce. It's a light blue-green, somewhat viscous, and smells a little like airplane glue. Its most important properties? It burns at a lower temperature than most flammable liquids and is extinguished more quickly than most flammable liquids when deprived of oxygen. She had a few ounces of it in a squat, wide-mouthed jar.

She showed me her three torches, which she makes herself. She takes a sixteen- to eighteen-inch dowel, about the circumference of a fat pencil, paints it black. Then she wraps lantern wicking three or four times around the top of the dowel and nails it in place with thin, tiny nails. It's very important to drive the nails deeply (but not so deeply they go through the top layer) into the wicking and into the dowel: You don't want the nails to get hot when you light the torch. The torch head is about the size of a golf ball. She puts a small candle on a plate, lays down another plate on which to put the torches, and that's all she needs. She dipped a torch into the secret sauce. You want it "squishy" but not dripping excess sauce. She lit it from the candle, held out her right hand, palm up and tapped the torch to it: For a few seconds a fairly large (maybe ten times the size of a candle flame) blue, wavering fire rose from her palm. She snuffed it (I never counted—four to five seconds?) by closing her hand. Gotta tell you: Very cool to see this, particularly for the first time.

She demonstrated several feats, my favorite of which was lighting her tongue on fire. I wondered how she timed how long she let a flame burn on her hand or tongue. Did she count seconds? No, "but you need to remember that when the secret sauce is burned up the fire will commence to burn something else, i.e., your skin." I kept thinking what a great picture it would be in the dark: A woman's face lit by a fire on her out-thrust tongue. Or a man. I told a friend I'd like a picture of myself with my tongue on fire. She said nowadays one could create the same effect on a computer; it would look just the same. I said I thought that might defeat the point. She then, smart woman, said something flattering about my tongue, and before I knew it, I'd promised not to set it on fire. I'll detail the fire-eating further when Karen initiates JB by revealing to him the secret sauce and teaching him to eat fire.

First, I had to go to Tijuana for a day. I'd heard there were fire-eaters there, and I was, in particular, interested in finding a twelve-year-old boy who breathed fire by night and often did a juggling act in parks during the day. He was called DragonBoy. DragonBoy used diesel fuel to blow his fire. I had learned earlier this important distinction: The people who fill their mouths with a flammable liquid and then spew it out and over a flame to create a dramatic fireball are not fire-eaters. They are called fire-breathers. I'm sure some people both breathe and eat fire, but fire-breathers don't put burning torches into their mouths. I'm sure those who both eat and breathe fire take special care to wash out their mouths thoroughly after breathing fire and before eating fire! In fact, flames should never come near a fire-breather's mouth, but they might if he sprays the liquid too slowly or it lacks the proper mistiness. Fire-breathing is considered easier. JB could already do that standing on his head: He wanted to eat it.

I wanted to find DragonBoy. My Spanish is poor, and I don't know Tijuana very well. So, I invited JB to come along. I'd get to talk to him more, and his Spanish was better than mine. Which meant we had about twelve badly-mispronounced words between us instead of four.

So, off we went. We knew we were unlikely to see anyone breathing fire in daylight, but we got to TJ about 3 P.M. to check some parks and to try to find DragonBoy juggling. When firebreathers do their business in Tijuana they must be quick about it. Sometimes they work the border's waiting lines, but mostly they set up at an intersection, and when the light is red they run out, blow some fire, try to get tips from drivers, and scurry off the street when the light turns green. They can't work a light, or anywhere, very long: The cops chase them away. We checked out a few parks where we'd heard the kid might be. No kid, no juggler, no fire. We walked and walked, often asking people with sign language and a few words. We knew *fuego* meant fire. I found out later that the correct Spanish word is *tragafuego*. Literally: To swallow fire.

Most people seemed to know what we were talking about and would say, Yes, Yes, on this corner, on that; Oh yes, the boy who juggles and spits fire. We walked and walked. Turns out JB didn't know Tijuana that well either, but we didn't care, we were on a quest, we were chattering away with each other. Near the end of a pretty run-down street we saw a few guys sitting on the curb shooting drugs. A few yards later, at a corner, a Tijuana police van with three cops screeched to a stop and braced us. They figured out pretty quickly we'd wandered into the wrong neighborhood. When we explained what we were looking for (their English was strong), one laughed, one rolled her eyes, and the third looked like he wanted to run us in for being dumb. They, too, gave us directions to where we might find DragonBoy.

It was getting dark; we felt our luck was bound to change when we saw two jugglers/acrobats in clownface working an intersection. While the light was red, one stood on the other's shoulders and both juggled, singly and with each other. They had about forty-five seconds to work, and another fifteen to cop some change. We talked to them, neither was DragonBoy, but they seemed to know exactly whom we were looking for and where he was. We followed their directions: Nada.

We asked taxi drivers. After a lengthy example of miscommunication, we figured out one taxi driver thought we were looking for an arsonist. He was more than willing to take us to one. Another cabby thought we were looking for a place where a woman set her nipples on fire. He knew of a place like that. No, *gracias*. We walked, we wandered, we ate a few meals, waiters would tell us, *Sí, sí*, you will find them here or there. Everybody had seen fire-breathers, and several seemed to know DragonBoy. We walked miles and miles, the only people in TJ searching for what we were searching for.

Let me tell you some other things about JB: He's a fun walking companion and raconteur. He's chipper. He's indefatigable. And regarding his imperviousness to pain: The day before our excursion, he had, while cutting a piece of thick plastic with a power saw at his machinist's job, shot a three-inch shard into his upper right groin. About the size and shape of "a small knife blade." He didn't notice he was impaled until its protruding end caught on the corner of a workbench. He pulled it out and debated whether to stitch it up himself or go to the doctor's. Once he learned his insurance would cover the visit, he went and contented himself with supervising the physician. On the trolley home from Tijuana, he was happy to show me the nasty little stitched-up wound.

You've guessed by now we never found DragonBoy. If we weren't looking for him, we would have found him easily. As we were walking up the ramp to the border, still on the Mexican side, I saw a quick, large gust of flame a few hundred yards away in the lines of cars jerking forward. A few seconds later: Again. I could barely make out the silhouette of the person blowing the fire. DragonBoy? We never knew. We kept walking across. JB bought a few Day of the Dead figurines as a birthday gift for his girlfriend. When asked at Customs what was in the bag he said just that and was waved through. We were probably in the minority, crossing late on a Friday night: Stone sober, carrying no mood-altering or other pharmacological substances, and utterly chaste. When the customs officer asked me if I were bringing anything back I said, "Only a headache and a sense of failure: I could not find an eater of fire." Without a blink, she waved me through.

I was a little disconsolate on the way back to San Diego but heartened by a promise JB made to me: He'd blow himself up tomorrow.

The next day he took me to a large indoor space, a small warehouse-like structure in an area I was asked not to disclose. When we went inside, JB excused himself and said he'd be right back. I assumed he went to the can. He was gone about ten minutes. I was looking at some pictures on the wall and turned to see him walking towards me, maybe twenty feet away. He changed his shirt, I thought. In mid-stride: KABOOM! I jumped about a foot in the air and about two feet back. I had to smack myself on top of the head a few times to get my heart back out of my throat and down to where it belonged. Smoke was everywhere, my ears rang, paper from the crackers was floating to the floor. JB grinned. I'd grown rather fond of the lad and thought it was time to pass on a little avuncular advice: "YOU CRAZY MOTHERFUCKER, DON'T EVER DO THAT AGAIN!" I calmed down a bit: "Or don't do it without some kind of advance warning—maybe ask each audience member to bring a doctor's note—and not without good insurance and a good lawyer. Somebody will have a heart attack! Somebody will be strapped and shoot you five times in the head!" JB looked at his left sleeve, which was burning at the cuff. He tapped it out as if he were mock-slapping the wrist of a naughty child. "Want to see me skewer my arm through a meat hook and then hang by it?" A perfectly reasonable question, given the circumstances. I said, "Not today, thanks." He was just kidding, though. He does skewer himself with different implements but "Hang by my arm from a meat hook? That would hurt," he said.

After we made plans for his fire-eating lesson the next day, I went back to the condo and called my cardiologist.

Karen invited JB and me to her house on a brilliant Sunday afternoon for JB's initiation into the brother/sisterhood of fire-eaters. There we met her husband, Eric Bakanic, also thirty-one. Eric's about six feet tall, lean, fit, and Bolivian born. Their house, in North Park, is compact, neat, and airy. We chatted for a while: An old professor (me), a young professor (Eric), a soon-to-be professor (Karen) and the Nutty Professor (JB).

Eric, who clearly adores his wife, not only loves to watch her eat fire, but also loves to watch other people who are seeing her eat fire, particularly for the first time. Eric does know the secret of the secret sauce. Karen didn't tell him for a long time and then let it slip by accident. Eric's response to my inquiry about this was: "But I've developed amnesia."

At one point in our getting-to-know-you conversation, JB described his butane/smoke/bubble feat. Karen said to JB: "It's not for me, like it is for you, an exercise in the imagination—what if I tried to do this, or that?" The "this or that" is the part of JB's psyche that pushes him to do things most of us would need hallucinogins to imagine or anti-nausea pills to watch. On a video tape of JB's club act, different people yell out, several times, "YOU SICK FUCK!" I loved the contrast: Sweet, learned, gracious Karen chatting with and about to teach JB—a sweet lunatic and autodidact—to eat fire. Another contrast was very evident when I transcribed the tape of this conversation: The refinement and good taste of women versus the goofy crudeness of men. Here's a snatch of conversation (verbatim but for a few stage directions, indicating tone). Me, to Karen: "JB does some really weird things." Karen: Giggles, nervously. Me: "He puts an electric drill up his nose." Karen: "Gosh," politely. Me: "He also pounds a spike up his nose." Eric: "Yeah!" Karen: "Wow." Just about any woman reading the above will know the tone of this "Wow," and why it does not take an exclamation point. Eric: "Isn't that called Blockhead?" (The technical name for this kind of sideshow act.) Karen: "Wow." Eric: "Spike and hammer!" JB: "Rocks and stuff too." Karen: "Wow." Eric: "I totally have to see this!" Karen: "Would anyone like some water, or juice?"

JB mentioned his self-skewering feats, and, while showing Karen scars from it, Eric suddenly remembered something: As a child, he'd occasionally take a needle and thread and carefully sew little patterns under the skin of his fingertip. He was surprised to remember this so suddenly, and he'd, of course, never told Karen. Can JB and what he does bring up, sometimes, from his and others' unconscious, something primordial, atavistic? Do the heebie-jeebies open up the back door to the monkey brain?

We decide to have the initiation/lesson in the garage because the back patio is too bright. While Karen was showing JB how she sets up the sauce, the candle, and the plate for the torches, she leaned towards him and whispered in his ear the secret of the sauce. JB, who has more than a layman's knowledge of incendiaries and flammables, looked a little surprised and then the "Oh, yeah, why didn't I think of that?" look came over his face.

She talked him through some of the basics. Rhythm and timing are important—dip torch, light torch (never let it touch wax of candle), tap lit torch on palm, let burn for a few seconds, close hand. How to stand when actually eating fire: One foot forward, head tilted back so torch head goes almost straight down the throat and the flame moves upward, away. *Never* inhale: That takes the flames down your throat and sucks in oxygen, making it burn even hotter. The technique is simple but hard to do. The basic human instinct about fire is: Don't put it in your mouth! But you must enclose your lips and teeth completely around the burning torch head and the dowel. You don't want to let the torches burn too long before you eat the fire: The dowel will get too hot. I kept wondering why no one seemed concerned with how hot the fire was. A regular torch fire would burn at about 2,000 degrees Fahrenheit. Sure, the secret sauce burns cooler, but it's still burning at several hundred degrees. When you've closed your lips and teeth around the torch head, you exhale "from your diaphragm" and blow a puff of air outward. Fire-eaters learn how to do this almost inaudibly. They don't want to give the impression the flame is blown out. It's not. That helps a little, but mostly the flame is extinguished by lack of oxygen. Remember, too, upon exhalation, there is less oxygen: Your body just used it to feed your blood.

JB is a natural. First of all, he's fearless. Two: As he said: "I've put a lot worse things in my mouth." He ate fire on the first try, but not flawlessly. His exhalation was too loud, and he couldn't yet close his whole mouth around the torch. He did, more or less, blow it out. But in a few more tries, he nails it. Karen taught him the tongue on fire trick. She said to JB: When you tap your tongue with the torch, you kind of "skwoosh" it on. This took him three times to nail: He could light his tongue easily enough, but he couldn't withdraw his burning tongue back into his mouth (could you?), so he'd give a kind of Bronx cheer and blow/spray it out. Fourth try he got it. JB was excited: He had some new material for his act, and I could tell he was already beginning to work out extensions, variations, twists, nutty perversions, with his new skill.

After he'd eaten one torch, I said I heard a little *ssssssst* sound. He said he'd shave, closer next time, trim his nose hair, maybe even lose the world's smallest beard, all of which got singed slightly. I brought up the sauce again. I wanted more information. Long-term effects? Karen said: "I still have all my taste buds." JB said: "You couldn't beat it out of me." Which I didn't doubt for a moment. I imagined JB in another century brought up on blasphemy charges before Inquisitors and suggesting to them more efficient ways to torture him, if only for his amusement and to save time and stress on the torturers. Then Karen added: "It is a carcinogenic substance." JB, I assume, considered this a plus.

Karen was a terrific teacher—patient, thorough, firm on the fundamentals, not cheap with praise. JB learned very quickly but was impatient. I understood what he meant when he told me earlier he could do sleight-of-hand tricks well, though "too fast." They have to be fast, I thought. But too fast can screw up the trick just as easily as too slow. I loved this dichotomy in JB: Recklessness combined with sweetness and sense of wonder. He does exhibit a child-like sense of wonder—but what he wonders about makes you wonder. The lesson over, it was time for JB to show us some of his feats. We had set up chairs in the open garage, our backs to the street. JB doesn't warm up much: He plugs in the drill, turns it on, and up his nose it goes. As he works it in—only six to eight seconds—he wriggles his nose a bit and makes a face similar to the face one makes when suddenly overwhelmed by a bad smell.

On the tape, Eric and I are hooting and laughing, and Karen says, "Wow." Again, every woman knows the tone. Then, he pounds the spike (he made it himself, stainless steel) into his nose. Then he pulls it out with the claw end of the hammer. What surprised me, but not Eric, about these feats was that the drill and the spike were angled so they went almost horizontally into his face, rather than upwards as I expected. What I saw as a pleasant surprise (the angle of the drill, the spike) and which I felt increased the impressiveness of the act, made Karen uncomfortable. The one word from the professors, over and over, usually with exuberance, sometimes a qualifier, and always with an exclamation point was "Cool!" Karen is not heard on the tape for quite a while—I think she excused herself. Then JB did his condom sniffing act, and Eric and I (Remember: We provide higher education for your children!) go nuts, laughing our asses off while JB snorts a condom in one quick inhalation, holds on to one end hanging out of his nose and works the other end out his mouth, then proceeds to pull it back and forth, in an action similar to someone buffing a shoe. He can blow the condom up, while it's in his nasal passages, so a huge bubble grows from his mouth or nose. He blew large condom bubbles out of both nostrils at one point. How he did that I don't know. Eric and I laugh and whoop. Karen says, "Wow." Either, she was there all along, or she'd gone and come back, I'm not sure. Now, she does excuse herself, graciously.

Eric (remember, he's a professor of linguistics) asked JB what it felt like, passing the condom through his nose and out his mouth. JB said only one part felt weird—where he could feel it pressing against something that caused discomfort. JB never studied what was going on up there in his nasal passage, but Eric did know: "There's a hard part, the palette, at the top of your mouth, and you can feel, with your tongue, behind it, it gets more soft and fleshy. That's actually a valve that closes off the nose passage from the mouth. It's called the velum. When you drop the velum then air can go from your lungs to your nose and also out your mouth. It's how we make different kinds of sounds, by opening and closing the velum, so what you're doing is opening it a little bit to get a passage. There are some nerves there that aren't used to being touched by anything but air." JB said, "Cool." Eric said: "That's cool, even though I know what's going on, that's very cool." He then suggested JB look at something called a mid-sagital chart or diagram. It's essentially a picture of a head cut in half (not a real head!) so one can see all the passages and connections. JB clearly liked the idea of a picture of a head cut in half.

Several minutes of the tape consists almost entirely of Eric and me howling with laughter. And, a little further back from the recorder (when he doesn't have something up his nose), JB is yelping too. The boys were being boys.

Laughter begets laughter, it's good medicine, I believe, so I listen to this part of the tape if I'm feeling too serious. There we were, on a beautiful Sunday afternoon: The professors, Eric and myself and JB (for whom a title must be invented by someone with an imagination better than mine), and we were three happy guys, one of us in love with a woman who eats fire (also happy but, at the moment, absent), another delighted he's learned a new skill to which he can add his own demented variations, and me feeling grateful, glad to be walking up and down on the planet. "Oh lucky life, lucky, lucky life," wrote the splendid American poet, Gerald Stern, "Oh lucky life."

SUFFER THE LITTLE CHILDREN

Cops like to tell stories. They're good at it. They're trained to think in specifics, precise observation. Atop an arrest report it says, "Narrative" right beneath "Officer's Report."

On one of my first days at the Chula Vista Police Department, I went with Agent Ruth Hinzman, Agent Phil Collum, and a uniformed officer, on what is called a child welfare check. Hinzman and Collum work in the Family Protection Unit (henceforth FPU) at the Chula Vista PD. Their main beat is child abuse and molestation, sex crimes, elder abuse. It was a return visit to this house to see if conditions had improved from the last time they were here, a week or so earlier, following up on a complaint that the children were inadequately cared for and possibly abused. The place was dead-rat dirty and contained little edible food. They checked the kids, told the mother to clean up the place and get some food. Told her they'd be back. This time, they came unannounced, at about ten A.M., and it took repeated knocking on both the front and side doors to rouse the occupants. When the mother finally answered the door and let us in, the conditions looked bad enough to me. The place smelled—of mold, urine, shadows, diapers, of a sad sourness. The woman's eyes seemed bleary and darkened to me. Bruises, I thought. Ruth told me later it was smeared make-up covering old bruises. Two of the children, a boy and a girl, dressed only in underpants, sat on the couch. Several loaves of bread, covered with huge spots of blue-green mold, were on a table just outside the kitchen door. A half-eaten fast food sandwich sat on the table. I noticed a poured, and then forgotten, glass of milk on a windowsill—a few inches of it evaporated, leaving a dusty, white ring around the inside of the glass.

Phil awakened the woman's boyfriend, who was sleeping in the garage. He sat with his elbows on his knees and his head in his hands, as if nursing a massive hangover. Ruth spoke to the woman. Phil checked the refrigerator for edible food and also the bathroom to see if it was operable and clean enough. I thought, given the way the place looked, that the kids would be scooped up, and removed on the spot. Instead, after explaining to the woman that they'd be checking (ditto Social Services) on her and the kids again, we left. When I asked, Ruth said that the place was much improved, cleaned up considerably. I said I couldn't imagine how it looked before, and Phil said something like: "You should have seen the place I went to once."

A few days later, he showed me the arrest reports he and another officer wrote about that call. The names and the addressees were blacked out. First, from the other officer's report. He and Agent Collum arrived at about the same time: "As I stood in the doorway, I observed trash and garbage all over the entire house that I could see from my vantage point. I could smell urine and several other smells that made me gag and almost throw up." The mother (there were four children living here) informed the officers that she didn't feel well. "She said she had eaten a lot of chocolate and was going to the doctor." Collum's report (he also took three rolls of film) commented on the smell too: "I was immediately bowled over by a powerful odor emanating from within the apartment. I saw that the entire floor surface was completely covered in dirt, filth, feces, and other debris." The first child he saw, lying naked in a fetal position on the sofa, turned out to be a three-year-old boy. "I could see marks on his back, which appeared to be green crayon marks. There were several of them, as though someone had been writing or drawing lines across his back." Collum stepped into the house: "I looked around and saw numerous insects flying through the air and crawling over just about everything in sight. The entire ceiling area appeared riddled with spider webs, spiders, and other insects, as did all the corners and walls of the apartment." The mother told Collum that a second child, a daughter, was in the other room. (The other two children were not at home at the time.) "I located the child in what appeared to be a master bedroom. She held her hands clasped together near her mouth with her elbows out. She was spinning with her torso back and forth as she sat. She appeared very stressed and extremely frightened. I called to her and tried to speak with her, but she was completely non-communicative." After Fire Department medical personnel arrived, they said it was too filthy to try to treat the mother and the children in the house so they moved outside. The mother signed a "consent to search" form, and Collum went back inside to take pictures and continue his report, which he was recording. It starts innocuously enough: "I saw a few toys, including a toy baking oven and other small items." Then follows a walking tour of Hell: "In several areas of the floor were piles of what appeared to be human feces and urine stains. I noted used diapers in the tens piled and strewn on the floor...while it appeared there had been food in the refrigerator at one time, those items were now completely non-edible, covered in mold and insects...when I looked at the bottom of the refrigerator I noted that it seemed extremely dark...upon closer inspection I noticed that the entire floor of the refrigerator was covered with dead insects, such that I could not see the bottom...piles of insects flowed from the floor to the refrigerator and onto the carpet area just beneath it...the sink appeared to be clogged with a liquid substance filling within."

He saw a big bag of cat food and an overflowing bowl of it, and a box where he surmised a cat recently gave birth to a litter. Agent Collum thought he might be walking on dead kittens (there were squishy spots) beneath the trash but later a neighbor told of the kids throwing a kitten against a fence, picking it up and tossing it again. The neighbor also reported the kids trying to hang a cat by the neck from a tree. The kids were taken to Children's Hospital, and when Collum arrived shortly thereafter, hospital staff informed him that the children were swarming with lice. One of the last lines of the report, referring to the little girl he found in the bedroom, is: "She was still completely non-communicative. The only word I heard her say throughout my entire contact with her was NO. She said this when one of the staff attempted to take a toy away from her."

Maybe this is not high narrative, but it sure tells the story. I've read many literary novels I've almost completely forgotten. This narrative I will never forget.

A cop for eight years, Phil Collum is thirty. Because the younger officers at the police academy graduate when they're in their early twenties, it's possible to be a seasoned veteran by thirty or so. He's a San Diego native and attended UC Santa Cruz. Tall and lean, he runs "at least twice a day" and works out religiously as well. He goes to bed about 8:30 at night and gets up at 4 A.M. He describes himself as one of the department's few real "computer geeks."

He and his colleagues see and smell things like the above on a more-or-less regular basis, that is, when they're not dealing with child molestation, rape, people beating up and robbing old people, etc. Not a happy job. Not one, either, without its rewards.

Agent Collum told me about a rape case he'd worked on. A man attacked a woman, beat her, and raped her with a foreign object in a ditch near her home. This was one of the rare "stranger" rapes—someone who knows the victim does the vast majority of rapes. Somehow, she managed to talk the rapist into taking her back to her apartment, where she knew, and he did not, that her roommates were home. She escaped by screaming the second she opened the door. Collum admired her courage and developed a good rapport with her during the investigation and through the rapist's trial. He was arrested only minutes after fleeing. She made an excellent witness. The guy got thirty-one years to life. He has to do at least twenty-four. That's one of the rewards. Collum called it "the 'one strike and you're out' law—for real offensive offences."

Agent Collum was the second man on the scene at the notorious Jenny Rojas murder case. He said all during the investigation he was OK, but at the trial, on the stand, when he looked at pictures of the murdered child, he nearly broke down: "Well, it's been emotionally difficult since then. Images that I'll never forget."

One of the things Collum was doing (each officer in the unit averages about forty-seven cases a month) on top of his regular police work was writing up a grant proposal to get some more computers for the unit. I thought: Cops have to apply for grants to buy equipment? Poets should apply for grants (and not get them—it makes them tougher), maybe scientists, graduate students…but not cops, the goddamn city or state should just give them what they need! Then I thought: No, I forgot, all the money goes to teachers and social workers. I was working up a little irony lather.

Ruth Hinzman, forty-one (could pass easily for someone a half-dozen years younger), is a fifteen-year police veteran and with the FPU four, two in an earlier tour and two and counting now. Like all officers, she spent several years on patrol. She's also worked traffic and property crimes. She has brown hair and soft brown eyes. Let me put it this way: If she worked a different unit and wasn't married, I might turn into one of those guys who confesses to every crime he reads about in the papers—if they let me confess to her. She has a seven-year-old daughter from a previous marriage, and was recently remarried. Around the FPU she has the reputation of being a disarming and expert interrogator. She once got a guy to confess to rape by saying to him things like: "You know, I don't consider what you did as rape, rape is a very harsh word. I saw how that girl was dressed—she probably wanted it. I'd call what you did more like vaginal trespassing." Guy says, "Yeah, that's what it was, trespassing." He's thinking—"Trespassing, that's only a minor misdemeanor, hell, I'll cop to that rather than rape." Too late, sucker, you already confessed to a felony: Rape. Vaginal trespassing is rape. Adios, you're on your way to a bid in state prison. Ruth will say to a guy: "I can see why she (a twelve-year-old) would want to have sex with you, you're a good-looking, sexy guy, and she came on to you, right?" The macho dork's (Ruth's most common word for offenders) ego kicks in, and he admits it: "Sure, I fucked her brains out, she loved it." Got you, moron. Being stupid isn't a crime but being stupid and a rapist is. Sex with a twelve-year-old is rape. (Note: I never heard these cops, or any others for that matter, use the word "perp." Most often offenders were referred to as dorks, bad guys, yahoos, and a few others not fit for family newspapers.)

Ruth was the only female agent in the unit at this time. Another, Sgt. Laura Colson, recently left to take a job as investigator for the DA in San Diego. I assumed, since many of the victims this unit deals with are children and women, that children and women (particularly after a rape) might be much more comfortable talking to a female cop. I didn't want to stereotype, and each time I heard one of the male cops speak to a woman or child victim, they did so with gentleness and patience. I asked Ruth about this. She said she tended to make people, in general, feel comfortable, and victims, particularly rape victims, often request to talk to a female officer about what happened to them. If she's not available, another female officer will be.

I also asked Ruth, as I asked most of the other officers with children, if working in this unit affects how they raise their own kids. They all used the word, "paranoid." All of them. And to each I said, "I'm sure you don't mean that in the clinical sense." What they meant was: They are super-vigilant. She said: "Say we go to Target and my daughter wants to look at Barbies. I stand there with her. I'm not gonna leave her alone. If I were a pedophile, that's where I'd be looking for victims."

Later she told a joke: Man comes home to find his wife enraged and throwing all his stuff out of the house onto the lawn, etc., screams at him, "You sonofabitch, you bastard, I just found out you're a pedophile!" Man says, "Why, sweetie, that's a very big word, pedophile, for a ten-year-old girl to know." (Note: Lest the reader's irony meter is off, or my timing: The joke does not make light of pedophilia, it makes, I hope, scathing fun of some men's notions that sex with children is an acceptable thing.)

One of the more common, ugly, and frustrating crimes the FPU investigates is date-rape, sometimes called acquaintance rape. This most often involves minors, girls twelve to sixteen, say. The suspects are usually young men, eighteen to early twenties. "The letter of the law is clear: If a woman says no, the action stops," Ruth said. But there is sometimes a sense of ambivalence. "A girl never deserves it, and girls and women need to do what we can to protect ourselves. We need to be cautious of our actions and our surroundings. We need to ensure we don't do anything that could lead to our victimization." She added, "The way I was brought up, you don't get yourself in a situation you can't get out of." Most of the time alcohol is involved. And, in recent years, Rohypnol, "roofies" on the street, have been used by men to knock women unconscious, after which they rape them. No one in the unit had heard of a case where a man was given Rohypnol and raped. It's a drug given to patients about to undergo major surgeries. (Note: Who, or what, in our psyches, in our culture, in the darkest pits of our souls, is it that allows a man, young or old, to believe sex with an unconscious woman could in any way be right or pleasurable? I ask of psychology: Does this indicate necrophilia is really a much more common deviancy than previously thought?)

But rape is not about sex, no matter what the situation, it's not about sex.

Most often roofies are slipped, like a mickey, into a girl's drink. Ruth mentioned one young woman who took Rohypnol willingly to see what would happen. She'd also been drinking. She asked the boys she was with, whom she'd just recently met, to watch out for her and not to let anyone take advantage of her. What did the boys do when she went under? You guessed it—they raped her. Wonder why this crime is frustrating and very difficult to prosecute?

I heard a story later about a case Agent Pike (you'll meet him soon) worked. A nineteen-year-old was picking up (using Daddy's Caddy) girls twelve to fifteen, taking them to his apartment above the garage at his parents' house and, after giving them drugs and/or alcohol, would rape them, often inviting a few pals to join in the fun. There were more than a dozen victims. (Note: If I had a son, and he did that to someone else's child, my shame would be unbearable.) He also videotaped these sessions, sometimes with, sometimes without, the girl's knowledge. The guy pled out, got only a year of local jail time (a lot easier to do than state prison time), served part of it, and walked. He did become, as does everyone convicted of a sex crime in California, what's called a 290 registrant. Meaning he has to register with his local PD, inform them of the slightest move ("If you move even across the hall on the same floor you have to come in and tell us," Pike said to one man who came in). If you move to California from out of state, you have to register. This gives some satisfaction to cops who bust their asses to bust a guy like the nineteen-year-old above who, more or less, got off scot free: "At least he has to be a 290 registrant for the rest of his life." Legislation is in the works to make it mandatory for all convicted sex offenders to provide DNA samples for a national data bank.

The FPU office is announced by one of those ubiquitous signs stamped in white on plastic meant to look like wood: "Sex Crimes," it says, and just below that, "Child Abuse." You take a left past a door with a bright red "Biohazard" sign on it (I never asked), and the first thing you run into is a big pink pig, then a cow (wearing a cowboy hat), a bear (wearing a red cap), and a duck. There are many more stuffed animals here, dozens of them (donated, mostly by cops) and scattered throughout the office. Lying across five staplers on top of a file cabinet: A very languorous bunny. There are also a few shelves of blankets and quilts. Agent Collum opened a drawer filled with baby food and diapers. And many more drawings by kids than normal in an office. There's one next to Collum's desk: A river and mountain and forest with "Hi Phil!" written on it. The kid, who was being interviewed by Child Protection Services, knew Phil was watching through a two-way mirror (children are informed of this when they're interviewed), and he was goofing with him. These drawings give the room some color, which is good because it's crowded, cluttered, low-ceilinged, and dusty.

The agents all have a desk, some partially closed off, cubicle-style, all very close together. The place is noisy, with talk and phones.

When several people were in the office, I usually sat at the end of a table jutting out to just about the center of the room. Questions, comments, wisecracks fly around. Somebody asks another agent if he speaks Spanish. "Only enough to get my face slapped," he says. One agent would ask a question of another or just throw it out to the room: What's his name that did this or that, or what's new with this case? Or Ruth stands up and reads a postcard from the unit's sergeant, Tro Peltekian, who's on vacation with his family in London. (Note: I interviewed a few of the agents in Peltekian's small office in the rear of the main room because it was quieter. On his desk was a small fountain with some stones in it, dry now and lacking its soothing sounds, a box of tissues, and a large bottle of Tums.) Kevin Pike is asking Phil for some computer help. An officer comes in from another unit with a question. Another officer stops by to say hello or to grab a cookie or a piece of cake somebody brought in. The goodies occupied the other end of the table where I usually sat. Again, breaking stereotype, it wasn't the women in the office—Ruth and Wendy (whom you will meet presently)—who always did this. Once there was a plate of sliced-up skinless chicken breast. Or was it some kind of sushi thing? Everybody knew it was Phil Collum who brought that. Collum, as the unit's health nut, got razzed if he ate a cookie or a piece of cake. One day, Agent Munch (he, too, you will meet soon) was going to have lunch with his grandmother, who lived only a few blocks away. She asked him if he wanted a tuna or a liver sandwich. Some mirth was made over those culinary options. I didn't know, when I first spoke to Munch, that there was a TV cop with the same name, which explained the odd look in his eye when I didn't comment on it. Lots of his colleagues, of course, needle him about this.

Often, if there's a particular question about a particular case, or name, or date, it's not one of the agents who answers. It's Wendy Manzo, the unit's administrative secretary, who plays an important role on this team though she's not a sworn officer. She's a zaftig strawberry blond with a huge heart, exceptional memory for detail, and the only person in the office who speaks fluent Spanish. Wendy has three children, a fourteen-year-old son, and daughters thirteen and eleven. As a survivor of domestic violence herself, Wendy, now divorced from the father of her children and the man who beat her, can empathize with women in this situation. She understands why women stay with a man long after they know the relationship is abusive and dangerous—fear: Of more violence, of poverty, fear that they may deserve it or are to blame. The last beating she took from her ex-husband happened during a pregnancy. Her three-year-old was watching.

Her official duties at the FPU include answering phones, getting information to Child Protection Services, clerical support, transcribing arrest reports, etc. Unofficially, she acts as translator, counselor to victims and her colleagues, information ("I do pay attention") keeper and sifter, and general Big Heart. After ten years raising her children (who accuse her of being "paranoid" in relation to their safety) alone, she's been in a new relationship for the past year or so. She said it took her awhile to get used to a man who is gentle, thoughtful, and caring.

It's true that almost all of the bad guys this unit deals with are guys, men. Women abuse and neglect children but very rarely rape or sexually abuse them. When these cases do happen, they seem to get a lot more attention. The recent LeTourneau case, for example. She was convicted of sleeping with, and having a child by, her thirteen-year-old student. She got out on parole, slept with him again, was caught, got pregnant again, and went back to prison. Is it because these cases are rare and unusual that they get so much publicity, or might there be other reasons too?

One kind of child abuse, recently given a name, Munchausen Syndrome by Proxy, is particularly disturbing. This is when a mother (men commit these crimes too, but in this case are in the minority) deliberately makes or keeps a child sick in order to get attention, sympathy, and even money for herself. In one infamous case, a woman whose child was chronically sick for years was kept so by the woman putting potting soil or coffee grinds into the child's IV unit. Before it was learned what was really going on, the woman and her child had been picked up by the media as a tragic human-interest story—poor, dedicated, single-mother bravely fighting the HMOs and the medical establishment to get proper treatment for her child. The public sent her thousands of dollars in donations. Some people were caught, on video tape, lying across their children's bodies to the point of nearly smothering them (you see their little legs kicking desperately) and then calling the nurse or doctor in and saying, "See, my child is having trouble breathing or is having a seizure!"

Who but us is there to pray for us?

My first day at the FPU was also the first day in this unit for John Munch, a twenty-nine-year-old officer, newly promoted to agent, who had applied for an opening and got it. Munch is about six feet tall, sandy haired, and almost handsome enough to play a cop on TV (I really didn't know there was a TV cop by that exact name) if he weren't a real cop, and could act. He's married and has a three-month-old baby. When he told me this, I said he didn't look tired enough for a man with a baby. He told me his wife's been cutting him a little slack regarding nighttime baby care and was letting him sleep on the couch for a few nights. He then remarked that this is the only time sleeping on the couch is a good thing. Even though he was the new guy here, Agent Munch (though Ruth was a close second) turned out to be the office wiseacre.

His first weekend at FPU he was on call, meaning if a crime

occurs off hours and it needs an investigator's immediate attention, he shows up. The call came about midnight, Sunday. Saturday his baby had a rough night, and this time he shared the duties. The next night he and his wife had gone to her high school reunion, and he'd been asleep about an hour when the phone rang. He worked traffic for a few years—if his phone rang in the middle of the night then: "I knew somebody was dead."

When I saw him Monday morning, he looked more tired than even a new parent usually does. He was reviewing a videotape of a victim who had been held against her will and forced to perform oral copulation on her boyfriend for about five hours. It was 3 A.M. Agent Munch questioned the woman with patience and in great detail. The story was not without its oddities. For example, the suspect had some serious wood problems: He couldn't get it up while he was forcing her to do this. He was popping porno videos in the VCR at the same time, but they didn't seem to help. The victim, in her interview, said they were hardcore porno films. During the alleged knucklehead's—Munch's favorite term for a bad guy—interrogation he said one video was "some kind of women-in-prison movie that was hers" and the other was: "What was the name of it? A recent major motion picture." Where lies the truth? Sometimes, but not always, in the middle.

With the suspect he wasn't as patient and gentle and seemed a little more tired—it was 5 A.M. Occasionally, he seemed somewhat confused, asked the guy "help me out a little here." The guy had priors for sexual assault and was also on probation for an involvement with a crystal meth operation. Munch was very tired but was also playing the guy—he knew the suspect knew (he told him) he was new to this beat, he knew the guy was very savvy. My hunch is Munch was doing a little Colombo number on the guy, i.e., Agent Munch *can* act, at least on the job. As we'll find out, all of the agents have this skill to one degree or another. The suspect was hyper. He kept asking what he was charged with exactly, and when Munch named them (false imprisonment, forced oral cop, a few others), the suspect wanted to know the numbers for those crimes in the penal code—so he could look up what he might be facing, try to figure the odds, etc.

From both the victim and the suspect, he learned there was another person on the scene, though not in the same room—a friend of the victim's, who wouldn't leave because she was afraid for her. They were in a small trailer home, and the witness was very close, heard a lot, looked in a few times. She heard some thumps "like somebody's head knocking against a wall." During one of these look-ins, the victim mouthed the words, "Call the cops," and that's what she did. Munch needed to talk to her and went to her place of work to do so. During this interview, which contradicted the suspect's story and confirmed the victim's, he learned that the suspect once allegedly held another woman friend of hers at knifepoint for a day and a half, during which he took photographs of her. She did not elaborate on the nature of the pictures, but an image of this guy and his tastes was beginning to form in Agent Munch's mind. Before talking to this witness, Munch wasn't very optimistic about the case flying with the DA. He suspected that the victim ultimately wouldn't press charges, which often happens. (And which did, too, in this case a few days later.) But this witness seemed reliable, and said she'd be willing to testify. She was afraid of this guy and afraid for her friend.

Munch decided he might also arrest the guy for the knifepoint deal. He'd go to the jail and arrest him again tomorrow, and I could come along. Since I am a lover of irony (it seems to me one of the few defenses in a hypocritical and insane world), I liked that invitation. I've heard of people being arrested while already in jail or prison, but I wondered how it actually worked. Did you walk up to a guy's cell and tell him through the bars he's under arrest and read him his rights? Does he get cuffed and then moved to the cell next door? Do you pull him out of lunch line and read him his rights? He's breaking up rocks in the yard, and you say, "Hold that hammer a minute while I bust your ass"? What does a guy's face look like when he's already in jail and he gets arrested again?

When we got back to the FPU, Munch ran this possibility by Agent Ron Lederle (who's coming up soon) who advised him not to do it, at least at this time. I'm not sure who was more disappointed: Agent Munch or myself.

On my first day at the FPU, I met Agent Steve Fobes, briefly. It was his day off, but he was in anyway "checking on something." He wore shorts, T-shirt, sneakers, and a baseball cap. He's tall, dark-haired, in his early forties, and has a bit of a baby face. So does Agent Munch, which he says helps him sometimes in interrogations. I only caught glimpses of Fobes for the next several days, but I heard plenty about him from his colleagues. "Like a dog on a pant leg," Wendy said, describing how he works a case. "He just never gives up," someone else said. The case he had now involved a fifteen-year-old girl viciously date-raped (vaginally, anally, orally) a few days earlier by three young men, eighteen to nineteen. "They tore her up pretty bad," he said. The girl, who had drunk several shots of tequila and some beer, remembered very little of the attack. When she was taken to the hospital, her blood alcohol level was 4.6, which should have killed her. The state record is 5.1, taken from a wino in L.A. The legal limit is .08. The doctor at the emergency room said she had a 50/50 chance. She lived. Steve was already pretty sure he knew who the guys were, but he didn't have enough yet to arrest them. He needed more witnesses who not only put them at the scene but also entering or leaving the room where the girl was raped. I went with him and Agent Kevin Pike, fourty-four, father of five kids, and an eleven-year veteran of the PD, to look for this witness.

Pike didn't go to the academy until he was thirty-three—before that he worked for many years in Chula Vista recreation, in some of the roughest parts of town and, as a result, knew a huge number of people, two and three generations, often, of families, African American, white, Hispanic, Asian. His knowledge of the city and its people is very useful sometimes—when he talked a huge 300-pound man out of fighting another cop by saying, "Hey, it's me, Kevin, you know me, calm down, calm down." And sometimes a pain in the ass, like when other cops come up to him and say, I just busted so-and-so, and he says he's a pal of yours. He told me one woman even said she was his sister, and "I don't even have a sister." Agent Pike is built along the lines of a bulldog, wears a brush cut, and in his younger days was a hotshot basketball player. He's not particularly tall, so I said to him: "You must have had a good outside shot." He smiled a little: "Sure did."

They knew the witness was at the scene, the witness knew they wanted to talk to her, but she was proving elusive, they both thought deliberately so. Something funny was going on that neither of them could put a finger on, but something funny was going on. We went to one address. She no longer lived there. We went to a few other places. Nothing. We went to another place. A woman answered. I could see someone's legs—jeans, sneakers—inside, sitting on the floor watching TV. They got the address of the potential witness's mother and stepfather. When we got in the car, Fobes said to Pike: "That was one of the guys," meaning jeans and sneakers. Meaning one of the alleged rapists. The guy already knew he was a suspect. Both agents were happy (though they did not speak to him) to remind him of their continued interest in him, and the case.

I noticed that every time we approached a house or apartment door Kevin would reach back with his right hand and just barely touch the bottom of his holster. (I never saw a shoulder holster—they all wore their weapons on their hips.) I meant to ask him if he was aware of this but never did. They always stood to the side after ringing a doorbell. Steve said it was because if someone looked through the peephole and saw it was a cop, they might not answer the door. I'm sure, also, because there's always the possibility some bullets or buckshot will blast through the door—even on seemingly low-risk visits like these.

Forty-two cops were murdered in the US in 1999, sixty-one in 1998, all with guns, save one who was killed by a car. It's always there, in the back of their minds. One afternoon Agent Munch blew up then popped his sandwich bag. "Shots fired! Shots fired!" he said with mock alarm. And then: "That's a little cop humor."

When they went to the next house, they spoke to the girl's stepfather, who happened to be an attorney. After saying the girl wasn't home and that he'd rather the girl's mother not talk to them, Steve and Kevin told him (as they'd been telling everyone) that she wasn't in any trouble; they just wanted to talk to her. Maybe she heard cops were looking all over for her. Maybe she figured it was time to tell what she knew, maybe her stepfather urged her to after talking with Fobes and Pike, and getting the sense these guys are not going away so you might as well go in there and get it over with. Not long afterwards she was sitting in the lobby of the PD. I don't know what happened to this case, but I'll tell you what: They didn't let it go.

If all of these cops are driven, are pit bulls when it comes to their work, Steve Fobes, then, is a wolverine. "I won't let them outthink me," he said. When he knows something is off, something isn't jiving with somebody's story, "the hair on the back of my neck just stands up." He says sometimes it's like being a parent—"How does Mom know what she knows? She just knows." He, too, is very protective of his own children. His son plays baseball, and Steve insists he wear his cap bill forward, no other way. Why? Because certain gangs wear their hats at certain angles—he doesn't want his kid, even for a moment, even from a distance, to be mistaken for a gang member. That's the hat rule. For several months he's been on the trail of a guy who killed a two-year-old. "It's just a matter of time," he said, "just a matter of time, we've got so many organizations helping out on this." It's easy to tell: Nothing personal (or is it, a little, for each of them? Most are parents), but Agent Fobes wants this guy bad.

Ron Lederle, another agent in the unit, has twenty years in law enforcement and the most experience in the FPU—he was here for four years earlier and is now in the second year of another four-year tour.

Officers in the Chula Vista PD work patrol for several years after they graduate from the academy, and then, as they pass tests and openings occur, they can be promoted to agent (which is equivalent to, and more-or-less synonymous with, the rank of detective) and serve for four years in one unit and then rotate back to patrol (but still with the rank of agent, and wider duties than regular patrol) until they move again to another investigative unit.

Lederle spent his first five years as a cop with the Coronado PD. He said: "That was a whole different ballgame there, like Mayberry compared to NYC." He's always impeccably dressed, in his early forties, wears his graying hair straight back, sports a neat brush mustache, and is fairly recently divorced, with a sixteen-year-old son. When he spoke of his son, who he sees six days a week, his eyes light with joy. At one point, he handed me a poem he'd written. It's about a young girl in the hospital in a coma after massive head injuries. The poem is in metrical quatrains, and the second and fourth lines of each stanza rhyme. It's heartfelt and compassionate. He's not ready to quit his day job and make a living on the poetry circuit (everyone who has tried has starved anyway), but how many cops (or how many grown men, is more the point) do you think would have the guts to write a poem like this?

One case that haunts Ron involved a special needs kid in foster care. The kid was normal in most respects but had to be fed intravenously—he couldn't digest food properly. At bedtime he gets hooked up to a machine that feeds him over eight hours. One night his caretaker decides to go out and leaves the boy with a person who doesn't know how to operate the apparatus—he was given cursory instruction. Result is kid gets fed in one hour, which normally would take eight hours. Result is the kid is dead. And died horribly. No criminal charges are filed. Only his license to provide foster care was revoked. Another child under his care had died before this incident. Ron's keeping tabs on the guy. His latest information puts him in Mexico—"Working in orphanages or some kind of foster care employment there."

I went with Agents Lederle and Munch one day to Children's Hospital, to the ward where children are taken if they are abused, molested, raped. Lederle has particularly good rapport with the people here. He was showing Munch the ropes, places, procedures. He introduced us to a doctor, some nurses, and a forensic interview specialist, a person trained specifically to interview children about what has happened to them. I looked into a room marked "Child Protection Examination Room 1." Near the examination table I noticed a large medical instrument I'd never seen before. It's called a colposcope, and it's used for examining and photographing even minute damage inside, say, a child's anus or vagina.

Not long after this I went with Agent Hinzman to meet Floyd Richardson, Senior Social Work Supervisor at the Children's Services Bureau, which is part of the Health and Human Services Agency. How the FPU works with the people at Children's Hospital and Floyd and his colleagues is one of the things that make this unit different from others. Agent Hinzman said at one point: "I consider myself a social worker with a gun." Another time she said: "I've cleaned up vomit. I've cooked breakfast for a man who couldn't do it for himself. It's not in my job description, but I do it." Floyd said he sometimes had to act like a police officer, but without a gun. Most crimes don't involve social workers. Normally, a crime happens, somebody is arrested, tried, found guilty or acquitted. When the issue is child abuse or neglect, it's extremely complicated, and to take a child away from parents, "you need proof that the child is endangered—an equivalent amount of proof to prove murder—danger for the child is the guideline," Richardson said when I asked: "Where's the line?"

Floyd Richardson is in his late fifties and has been a social worker for twenty-seven years. He's of average height, carries a little extra belly and wears a substantial mustache. At the nape he wears his close-cropped hair a little longer—my guess is he puts it in a tiny ponytail when not at work. Floyd is legendary among social workers and cops in the San Diego area—for his concern and involvement with children both on the job and with track and field events, and in the martial arts. He's also highly regarded for his concern about the training and safety of social workers. He'd recently received the Jay Hoxie Award for "a compassionate commitment to children." He didn't tell me that, Ruth did. I thought: When all is said and done, when it's time to go wherever we go when we die, that would be a pretty good quote, honestly earned, carved on anybody's stone. A little later I learned he also holds a third degree black belt in Tae Kwon Do, which explained why he moved with such ease and grace. It also seemed like a good skill to have in his line of work.

The first Society for the Protection of Children was established in New York City in 1875. A child, Mary Ellen Wilson, was brutally abused by her caretaker. A citizen, unable to get help for her from any public agencies, convinced the American Society for the Prevention of Cruelty for Animals (already well-established) to provide assistance because Mary, as a human, was a member of the animal kingdom. The ASPCA did assist her, and soon thereafter legislation was passed to protect all abused or neglected children. By the 1920s there were 250 private, non-profit groups involved in providing assistance for families and protection through the courts for children. During the 1960s a great deal developed regarding the country's response to the maltreatment of children. A major step was created when "reporting laws" were passed in every state, meaning that every citizen was mandated to report child neglect or abuse—not just doctors, teachers, cops, but you, me, every citizen.

On Floyd Richardson's first day on the job—wearing a tie, carrying a clipboard—he's sent to the waiting room by his supervisor to talk to a woman who'd gone to the police first and from there was sent to Social Services. She was agitated and, Floyd figured, stoned. There was some problem with her grandkids, her daughter, the more she talked the more agitated she became. She knocked her huge purse off the table. Out spilled a large quantity of pills and a fully-loaded .357 magnum handgun. A big gun. Floyd grabbed and emptied it. "Graduate school did not prepare me for that," he said. He told me 300–400 social workers are assaulted each year nationally. In Sacramento, not long ago, a man shot a social worker and gave the gun to another social worker on the scene. In L.A., a social worker was assaulted, kidnapped, stabbed. It turned out it was arranged by one of her clients, a fourteen-year-old girl. He gave me a document detailing dozens of other specific incidents and which contains a list of recommendations, ten of them about training and safety issues. Number seven struck me: "Child Protection Services workers need training and guidance on steps that can be taken to shield their own families from vengeful actions by distraught clients. In small communities where it is easy to identify and locate a worker's family, training and information should be available to the worker's spouse and children."

I asked how the process of determining if a child is in danger begins. In a nutshell, a call comes in on the hotline: So-and-so is beating, abusing a child. This referral is cross-reported to the cops. The cops check it out and see if any laws are broken. The social worker checks it out and determines if the child is in danger. "Children get hurt without the law being broken…sometimes," Floyd said, and added, "It's black and white for the cops, gray for us. A social worker needs an education, life experience, and a philosophy to fall back on, an idea of what things should be." I asked him how things have changed since the 70s. "In those days sometimes you could help change things just by mere presence. People were more afraid of social workers than cops. It used to be a stigma, now it's no big deal."

Who else, except for a judge, has to make calls like this on a regular basis—whether a child stays with a parent or is removed from the home? And if he stays, is he safe? I kept thinking about the difficulty of that decision, what must go on every time Floyd has to make that call. I asked him about these decisions. "Torn" was a verb he used a few times. He gave me a "for example": A child ten to twelve is removed from the home. At age eighteen, he goes home to family: "He's alive, earlier he couldn't protect himself, now he can." And then he said: "The best place for a child is in the home if the home is safe. You don't get a lot putting a child in an institution."

Floyd has assembled something called the "Child Abuse Manual." Part of it relates to burns and how to tell the difference between an accidental burn and one inflicted upon a child deliberately. Burning children by immersing them in scalding water is not unusual, probably because people think they can get away with it, that it's easier to claim the injury an accident. One illustration in the manual describes what is called "the doughnut." If a child, say, is accidentally set in a tub of water too hot for it, the child screams and the adult, although guilty of being an idiot for not testing the water, snatches the child right out. The burn on the child's bum would show a fairly small doughnut hole—he won't be burned as much around the anus. If a child is deliberately put in scalding water and held there or pushed down, that doughnut hole will be squashed, with a larger circumference.

Ruth told me about a case where a boyfriend taking care of a girlfriend's baby placed the baby in scalding water and left the room "to do a few things." The baby screams and screams. The guy comes back. The baby's unconscious, underwater. The water is still too hot—too hot for him to put his hands in it to remove the baby! The baby died. The man, I hope, will fry.

The handbook includes all sorts of things you don't want to think about: "Spiral" fractures, a type of fracture that occurs when a child's arm is twisted until it breaks, splinters. This is the only (99%) way this kind of fracture happens.

I asked Floyd what he did to get away from his work. "Certain movies you don't see. TV programs. Can't really turn it off but can, kind of…I watch a lot of Disney. Always that type. I officiate track and field events. Martial arts." I asked him how he dealt with potential violence: "Cautiously." And I needed to know what kept him going, knowing what he knows. He said, "I know I absolutely made a difference in a child's life. Some things ugly are gonna happen. I know children are alive because of something I did. I run into a woman in the market, twenty-or-so years old. She doesn't recognize me. I recognize her, now all grown up, taking care of herself. She's alive."

Just about every member of FPU said a similar thing when I asked them the same question: "There are kids walking around today who wouldn't be alive." And fewer kids damaged forever by being molested, abused, raped.

I went with Agents Lederle, Pike, and Fobes while they

arrested a man for molesting his girlfriend's child. The child of *one* of his girlfriends. They arrested him at his and his wife's house. Ron explained to me that, in this case, because they didn't have a warrant for his arrest, the man needed to agree to step outside his house. Once he's outside his house he can be, with just cause, arrested. Ron used the word "ruse" in telling me that often cops say things to suspects that are not true. Ruth used a word, tongue-in-cheek: "Fibs." She gave me an example: A patrol officer knocks on a guy's door and tells him his car was broken into and he needs to come outside to identify his property. Surprise! If you don't take the bait? Some cops wait and make sure you don't leave. Other cops go get a warrant. Then they come back and arrest you in your house. Kevin Pike said, "We tell 'em all sorts (during interrogations) of things, we got this, we got DNA, we got a witness, etc." Ron goes to the door with Kevin. I stay with Steve, who watches the back. Ron notices the guy's wife inside when he answers the door and, figuring he doesn't want his wife to hear what's going on, asks him if he'd mind stepping out onto the patio for "just a second, I only have a few questions." Next thing the guy knows he's putting his hands behind his back, click-click, and he's off to jail.

A tool they use and consider more reliable than polygraph testing is called Voice Stress Analysis. A subject is asked questions over the phone, and the machine can, essentially, read lies in a voice. One agent claimed it was 98% accurate. Although its results, like a polygraph, can't be used in court, it helps cops in their investigations. They also use a technique called "a controlled phone call." I won't go into this in any detail, but here's a tip: If you've date-raped someone and she calls you and wants to discuss the incident, go right ahead and converse honestly with her.

Another kind of abuse, of elderly people, is a problem that's being aggressively addressed in San Diego County by both police and Social Services. If you watch local television, you've noticed a great number of public service announcements about elder abuse—as in neglect, physical abuse, and what is becoming more and more prevalent, "fiduciary abuse," i.e., ripping off old people, most commonly relatives, who have access to an older person's savings.

In some places, judges are trying what is usually known as "alternative sentencing." How about this: If a person is convicted, by a jury of his peers, of stealing from an old person and the result is serious deprivation for that senior citizen, then that person (after restitution) must wear a dunce hat and a sign around his/her neck for a certain period, saying something like: OUT OF GREED AND SELFISHNESS I STOLE FROM MY 87-YEAR-OLD MOTHER. MY OWN MOTHER! MAY SHE AND MY FELLOW CITIZENS FORGIVE ME.

I guess that is a little unusual, but stealing from or abusing an old and vulnerable person is odious and worse than "unusual" and wearing a signboard admitting that crime not half as cruel as the crime itself.

Rape, child abuse and molestation, elder abuse: Ugly crimes. A few of the people in the FPU said to me things like, "After working here, property crimes, car theft, don't seem so important. That's what insurance is for." The majority of the crimes investigated here don't end with the act. A child molested has a much greater chance of becoming a molester as an adult. The emotional and psychological damage (even if justice is done to the guilty party) is life-long. A rape victim, even if she sees a cell door close on her attacker for many years, even if she has the best therapy in the world, is forever affected. What must an older person feel, knowing they brought into the world the person who stole every dime they saved to live, with some dignity, in their later years?

I have a picture of Steve Fobes and John Munch I took on my last day at FPU. In office banter the day before, Agent Munch said that he'd been somewhat of a wild boy as a teenager. When he turned eighteen, his father changed the locks on him, and after a few months sleeping on friends' couches and in garages, he saw the light. A few years later he was at the police academy. Both were on the way out the back door when I asked them to hold a second for a picture. Fobes was bouncing on the balls of his feet a little—he wanted to get going. Maybe they were off to bust the date-rape yahoos. He's wearing a suit and tie. Either he was on his way to court, or he wanted to look particularly sharp when arresting someone. Munch was tieless for the first time since he came to the unit, wearing a gray shirt. They're smiling sweetly. They had places to go, people to arrest. They had work to do.

If you hurt or neglect or molest children, if you rape, if you hurt and steal from elderly people and you live in Chula Vista, CA, the people of the Family Protection Unit would like to meet you. In fact, they will meet you, sooner or later. They will reach out and gather you in, and, if they have the evidence they need, they will pass you on to other people (judge and jury) who, if they find you guilty, will put you in a place where you will not be safe. For a long, long time. If you do these kinds of crimes in Chula Vista, here, again, is the list of people who will be knocking on your door: Agents Collum, Fobes, Hinzman, Lederle, Munch, Pike. And when they're back from vacation: Agent Brown and Sgt. Peltekian. Wendy won't be at your door, but she'll be in the office, and she'll never lose your file. If you do not do these kind of crimes, or if you have a child or an older parent, or if you know a child or an elderly person, or if you once were a child and hope to be an older person, if you know someone who has been a rape victim, if you are a citizen with one dollop of gratitude, then it's to these cops, these social workers and hospital personnel, you might say: Thanks for doing what you do.

Hyp-no-tized

Some people believe God to be the first hypnotist: He put Adam to sleep and took out a rib to make Eve. It would have hurt, and God had yet to invent the guy who invented chloroform. It's a leap. Today, hypnotism is used, in some cases, as an alternative to anesthesia—in dental work and even serious surgeries. I've heard, but have been unable to verify, that two recent heart surgeries were performed under hypnosis rather than anesthesia. More and more, the medical establishment is accepting, even encouraging, alternative therapies. Law enforcement utilizes hypnotism—most commonly in helping people recall crimes they've witnessed, etc. It's a form of entertainment. Therapeutically, it treats an array of conditions/addictions/phobias. Steve Piccus, whom we'll meet later, treats narcoleptics and somnambulists (I wish I'd asked him if he knew any narcoleptics who were also somnambulists), does suicide intervention, teaches pain-management techniques, and more—all with hypnosis.

Most people know the term "animal magnetism." Its connotations now have little to do with its original meaning. When we use it today, it means, when applied to a person, usually male, he holds a unique and inexplicable power, something that makes him particularly attractive to the opposite sex. Though it wasn't his own coinage, the word came into being because of Franz Anton Mesmer, who was born in Austria in 1734. It's from Mesmer that we also get the word "mesmerized," which has connotations similar to animal magnetism. Mesmerized: Fascinated by another to such a degree as to be under a mysterious power.

Mesmer, a doctor, meant something else entirely. In a nutshell,

Mesmer believed the sun, moon and fixed stars affect each other and cause tides (like oceanic tides) in a subtle fluid, an ether, which he believed existed in the atmosphere and pervaded the entire universe. These atmospheric tides, when thrown out of whack, are the cause of all disease, especially of the "nerves." Mesmer believed this interrupted, or lost equilibrium, which is present in all healthy humans, could be corrected by moving magnets over the body in certain ways. He called his theory "Animal Magnetism." Later, he believed that his hands contained the same powers as steel magnets. He did not, however, give up magnets completely. One of his treatments called for a large oak tub, filled with magnetized water and iron shavings. Several iron bars poked out of the tub, each one grasped by a different patient. His treatments were popular (using the tub, he could treat many patients at once) and sometimes successful. He believed there was only one disease. And one cure: His.

He spent most of his adult life in France and enjoyed, for a time, the support of Marie Antoinette. Most other physicians considered him a quack. He made a fair amount of money, but by all accounts, he was sincere. He treated the poor for free. The medical establishment abhorred his theories and determined to take him down. And they did, officially, with committees, experiments, and reports by imminent doctors, who all dismissed his claims. All but one, a Dr. Deslon, a highly-respected court physician. Deslon believed fully in the phenomena of Animal Magnetism, but did not believe it had anything to do with magnets. Deslon believed it worked (sometimes) via the imagination of the patient, by what we would now call "suggestion." Or: Hypnosis.

Mesmer was adamant that his treatments had nothing to do with the imagination and adopted a "thanks, but no thanks attitude" towards Deslon. Mesmer continued his work. The disdain of the medical establishment was water off the back of a double-greased duck. He moved out of Paris to the fashionable resort of Spa and continued his work. Most of the money he made he put back into promoting his theories. Eventually, twenty hospitals, called Societies of Harmony, were built in major cities all over France. This annoyed the medical establishment, but there was nothing they could do about it. The King of Prussia begged Mesmer to settle in Berlin. He declined, so the King sent a man to apprentice himself to Mesmer, and later, the King appointed this person "Professor of Mesmerism in the Academy of Berlin." (Does this professorship and the Academy of Berlin, still exist?) A hospital, where Mesmerism was the only form of treatment, was built in Germany.

Mesmer's last years were peaceful. He owned a canary that lived in an open cage in his bedroom. Each morning the bird flew out and landed on Mesmer's head and then awoke him with a song, which would not end until Mesmer was up and dressed. He could put the canary to sleep with a light touch of the hand and wake it up again by stroking the feathers in the opposite direction. He played his harmonica and still treated poor people for free. He died at night in February of 1815. When dawn broke, the canary did not fly to Mesmer's head. The bird, in fact, never sang or ate again, and soon died.

Mesmer went the way of his canary still believing it was a kind of magnetic field that produced cures. Little did he know he would be considered, one day, the father of hypnosis. Actually, I prefer to think of him as the accidental grandfather and Dr. Deslon, the father. The word "mesmerized" that has come down to us should be "deslonized."

I'd been interested in hypnotism for some time. Probably because I'm a born skeptic, and I didn't quite believe it worked but had heard of its efficacy from enough people over the years to know there must be something to it. My daughter, for example, suffers from terrible headaches, just as I did at her age. She was taught some self-hypnosis techniques by a hypnotherapist, and it helped her a great deal. I'd spoken to law enforcement people who use hypnosis forensically. I knew people who had tried it to quit smoking and to lose weight. I knew enough to know that the stereotypes—the hypnotist swinging a watch in front of a subject's face and saying, "You're getting *sleeeeepy*," or the night club act where a shy librarian jumps up and down on one foot, flaps her arms and barks like a seal, were just that: Stereotypes. Still, I was skeptical. Could I be hypnotized?

I'd give it an honest shot. I'd get hypnotized up and down, inside and out.

I went to see Eric Kand in Pacific Beach. He's a practicing hypnotherapist, certified, experienced, personable. I had a specific issue I wanted to address. The exact nature of that issue is between a man and his hypnotherapist.

Kand is in his early thirties. He's trim, immaculate—he brushes his teeth between appointments—and passionate about his profession. We met at his small office about a mile from the beach. We went to lunch. He was the first hypnotist I talked to, and I had a lot of questions. I knew he had done entertainment hypnosis. I needed to know how a hypnotist got people from an audience of strangers to come up on stage and do outrageous or silly things. Imitate a chicken. Or sing like a member of the Village People. Actually, it's not the hypnotist who really makes this happen, it's the subject him/herself. First of all, someone under hypnosis never loses consciousness and won't do anything they wouldn't do otherwise. If you want to hypnotize a woman into going to bed with you, it won't work unless she wants to go to bed with you.

A stage-show works like this: The hypnotist calls maybe thirty people on stage and attempts to drop them all into a trance. This is done mostly verbally, and rarely with a pocket watch or one of those spiral, twirly things. He sends back to their seats those who do not initially respond. It helps, and most are, if the hypnotist is a student of human nature, has intuitive and empathetic powers.

The hypnotist looks for the most appropriate subjects, weeding out people who he thinks are faking, or not sober enough, while, at the same time, trying to find the ones not afraid to have fun, the ones willing to be silly. The subjects must want to be hypnotized. They are in a state of deep relaxation and glad to be goofy. Eric told me that you'd prefer not to give a hypnotist show to a room full of accountants or lawyers. The best groups are junior high or high school or college students. People at a convention away from home. Less inhibited crowds. The point is fun, laughs. The last people on stage are the most susceptible to hypnosis. Yes, they are conscious of what's going on. Yes, they are in a trance and open to suggestion. Hypnosis: A state of *deeeeeep* relaxation. The hypnotist gets you there by telling you to go there. It's not that some people can't be hypnotized, it's that some people don't *want* to be hypnotized.

The trance state (what it's called when one is hypnotized) is very common. We are each in and out of trance states every day. Daydreaming and all its variations (lost in a book, lost in a movie, lost in sex) is a trance state. Intense, highly-detailed daydreams are a very common form of trance. I'm not sure, for example, what an accountant daydreams about. Or an engineer. I teach at a university crawling with engineers of all kinds. A joke I've heard several tell on themselves: "Why do people become engineers? Because they don't have enough personality to be undertakers."

It makes sense that younger people are good subjects for stage hypnosis: They're all kings of daydreaming. I still remember in great detail an afternoon-long daydream that involved me firing a machine gun at Japanese Zeroes strafing my grammar school. No matter that I lived in inland Massachusetts and the war had been over nearly a decade. Needless to say, I shot them all down and was awarded a medal the next morning after we said the Pledge of Allegiance. And ditto, needless to say, a girl I had a crush on smiled at me. She looked exactly like Annette Funicello. I asked Eric if he had many kids as hypnotherapy clients. He said no, "because they're already in a trance!"

Did Eric feel there was anything contradictory about doing both stage shows and practicing hypnosis as a legitimate form of therapy. No, the stage show is fun, and it's a way of advertising his therapeutic side. It's "another line in the water." He meant this pragmatically (it's a business, it's how he earns his living), and he believes in the possibilities of hypnosis to help people, to help heal people, and any way he can get the word out, he will. I asked Eric about some of the things people came to him for. He said first that hypnosis was often a last resort: "People have run through medical doctors, shrinks, voodoo doctors not in the yellow pages before they come to a hypnotist." He also told me he rarely has more than three sessions with clients. Other hypnotists said this too. If they can't make at least a dent in a problem in three sessions, then they probably can't help. I wish the shrinks I've seen in my life made the same claim! I'd have a lot more money in the bank now. Eric summed it up this way: "Talking, talking, talking, and never moving." He also made it clear hypnotism's not a magic bullet. You don't get hypnotized and suddenly drop fifty pounds. Helping people quit smoking or lose weight are his bread and butter, but he also treats clients with social phobias, fears of flying, particularly since 9/11. After 9/11, he treated a client who had to commute weekly to Saudi Arabia. He said he not only helped the person to get over the fear of flying to that part of the world but also to enjoy the trip! He treats people who have a fear of public speaking. Public speaking is the average person's second greatest fear, coming right after death.

 A huge, soft, leather chair dominates Eric's office. It was like sitting in a large bowl of warm chocolate pudding. I came to call it "The World's Most Comfortable Chair." Eric said he shopped carefully for it: It's one of the few pieces of equipment a hypnotist needs. I think I dropped into a quarter of a trance as soon as I sat down in it and before Eric even opened his mouth. The curtains were drawn. He played a new-agey music—barely audible. I prefer New Age music *inaudible*.

 I told him my issue. He said it was like "a pocket of poison that needed to be popped." Like popping a pimple, I thought, which we all know leaves a red welt, which is much better than an active pustule. He takes, and encourages his clients to take, an aggressive approach in confronting an issue: "Bring it on, don't avoid the issue, challenge it to see if it's real. Sometimes you have to throw a couch off a roof to see if it breaks." I think he was glad to hear I didn't need to quit smoking or lose weight. A few minutes later I was in a trance, and this is how he got me there.

 As I said: Just sitting in the chair was the beginning of my induction—another word for being hypnotized. The client sits about two-thirds reclined, a little more than in your LazyBoy to watch a movie. Your ankles must remain uncrossed. I found this annoying and had to be reminded several times to uncross them. My natural inclination, when lying flat on my back, is to cross them. You also must let your hands lie by your side. My natural inclination is to cross my arms over my bottom ribs.

He asked me to put my hand, palm down, on his hand, held palm up. He asked me to press hard on his hand. Two or three times. And then he said, "Sleep!" I was paying attention to his voice as he dropped me into, and while I was in, a trance—its rhythms and cadences, his inflections, pacing, etc. The voice: The hypnotist's most important tool. Eric, sometimes alternately, sometimes at the same time, sounded like a radio announcer, a soothing, soft-speaking counselor, a stern teacher, an ardent coach, a preacher, an intimate friend. The speed, pitch, level of loudness or softness varied and were all done with purpose and good timing, shifting from one tone to another, waxing a bit dramatic, then toning it down. There was room for variation, for improvisation.

He asked me to squeeze my eyes shut. Then let go. Then squeeze them tighter, then relax, all without opening them and until I feel I can't open them. Then he told me to bring up my issue as an image and to try to make the feeling around the image rise from inside and travel down my legs and up my arms. Remember me saying I was a skeptic? I still am, but goddamn if I didn't feel and see the issue. He took me back before the most recent and painful manifestation of it. To an earlier manifestation. And then to one before that. Then to one I had no previous conscious memory of. He had me describe these scenes in the present tense. This was when he was stern: If I used the past tense, he insisted I keep it in present tense. All of these but the last had come up in conventional shrinkage, over many sessions, which always ended with me writing a check and saying: "See you next week." Eric had run me backwards through this ugly knotted rat's tail in about twenty minutes. Even though my issue occurred more recently, he asked me to step back from these memories and to speak as an adult to the child in the images. He told me to hug my child self. This is the only time I ever felt a twinge of the hokey. The whole "embracing the inner-child" pop-psychology fad came rushing back to me. Pop-psychology always annoyed me. So instead of hugging my inner child, I nodded gravely at him. And he returned the nod, as if he knew what he was in for. We were near the end of the session. Before Eric brought me out of the trance (by snapping his fingers!), he told me that when I left the office and saw the color red I would be filled with a sense of peace and well-being. I remember thinking: "Uh-huh."

    I left his office a few minutes later and looked to my left. There was a stoplight on red. It was the deepest, richest, creamiest, most evocative red I have ever seen, and it filled me with joy! I decided to walk to the beach of Pacific Beach—I'd never been there before. I saw a red pickup truck go by: Joy. I stopped to look at some rather bedraggled red flowers for several minutes, very happy. When I got to the beach I saw—it jumped out at me—a very loud red-and-yellow shirt. Way too loud for me. Possibly the world's ugliest shirt. I had to buy it and did and put it on right there on the beach and didn't (I swear, except to shower, and then only once!) take it off for three days, including sleeping in it. When I told Eric what happened after I left his office, he smiled and said, "I know."

    In the second and third sessions, he took me back to the examples of this issue coursing through my body, but this time he had me put spigots at the tips of each finger and toe. I know that sounds a little weird, but there they were, vividly, in my imagination, ten little silver spigots at the end of my extremities. Then he took me on a little trip that I didn't remember until I listened to the tape of this session. He had me imagine that all the negative issues in my body were like black, gooey tar, something I needed to get out of my body. Then, he had me imagine that a great light was entering my body from the top of my head. Then, he told me to open the spigots. Next, that the light was moving through my body and pushing all the tar and its toxicity out of the spigots. I was gradually filled with light as my fingers and toes oozed their goop. I could even smell it: Like day-old vomit, like a vulture's bowels. Goddamn if I did not feel a tremendous sense of relief. I say goddamn.

Next, he switched to a repetitious litany that seemed to have a sense of structure, and emphasized forgiveness—of others, of myself. Then he moved on to a similar riff on gratitude. These basic tenets are not new—they're the foundation of many religions, many twelve-step programs; hell, they're a part of the common sense we should all learn on our journey, but this time they made not only logical sense to me, but I also felt them in my body. Emily Dickinson, arguably the greatest American poet ever, said that her test of a real poem was, if reading it, she felt as if the top of her head had been taken off. She was speaking hyperbolically, metaphorically (poets tend to do that!), but she meant that the best poems don't only enter us cerebrally; they affect us physiologically as well. A. E. Housman put the same feeling in a slightly different manner: He said if he read an authentic line of poetry while he was shaving, he would cut himself. I was feeling something along those lines.

After Eric brought me out of the trance, he explained to me that for the effects to last I had to do homework, I had to re-imagine my images, I had to continue to practice forgiveness and gratitude. He taught me a technique using accupressure points and the repetition of certain phrases I could use if the negative, obsessive thinking returned big time. I wanted this issue to stop renting so much space in my head. Hypnosis helped. The issue did not disappear completely, but it was diminished, and the techniques helped keep it away when it lifted its ugly head to take a bite out of my ass. It was also clear to me—I could feel this in my body—that the hypnosis did not just cover up or mask the issue. Its pain was diminished, the pockets of poison were reduced to the proportions of pinpricks, when, before, they had gone through me like swords first slathered with the saliva of a Komodo Dragon.

Eric Kand told me about another San Diego-area hypnotist

named Eric Von Sydow. I did a little research on him and found out that he often works with a hypnotist named Steve Piccus (he's coming). I heard them referred to as "the Penn and Teller of hypnotism" and, equally interesting to me, "the bad boys of hypnotism."

I met with Von Sydow first. He's in his early thirties, about five eight or nine, dark-haired, and massively built. I had heard him described as "stocky." Not true at all: He is ripped, clearly has tremendous upper-body strength. He lifts weights about five times a week and had the biggest biceps I've ever seen live. His physical strength comes in handy sometimes at his night job: He's head of security at a strip joint not far from the airport. He likes the work and refers to it as his personal laboratory to study human behavior and dynamics. What he employs more often than his strength on the job are his hypnosis skills. He uses them to both deal with obstreperous patrons as well as some of the difficulties the dancers experience.

Von Sydow is a San Diego native who became obsessed with hypnosis and other healing arts in his teens. Like Kand, Von Sydow has done stage hypnotism. He refers to it as "sleight-of-mouth." It's not easy. On his third show ever, "I put nobody under. At least those people knew it's not fake." As a young man, he did some serious searching, studying massage, herbalism, metaphysics, story-telling, and shamanism. He experimented with mind-altering substances. He ran naked through the hills in the desert; he buried himself up to his neck. He participated in Dadaist-like pranks. He was "training my senses to create a richer texture to consciousness." He also told me (he is now stepfather to two teenagers), "I think I freaked my parents out during this time. My apartment looked like Willy Wonka's house."

In collaboration with the composer, Denver Clay, Von Sydow (using his stage name, Hypnotica) recently produced a CD called *The Sphinx of the Imagination*. It's a kind of "sound odyssey into greater possibilities." They worked on it for 10,000 hours, over many years. It's part story, part music, part allegory, part sound effects, and part hypnosis. Its intent is to "rewire and expand the listener's perceptions." I'm wary of these kinds of claims, but I listened to it three times, in total, and found it relaxing, moving, and, well, mesmerizing.

He agreed to let me tag along with him one night at the strip club so I could observe him in action. Sometimes writers have to make sacrifices for their work.

We went to the club together. The other security people and the dancers knew I was with him, knew I was writing an article, so I had more ready access and wasn't seen as a customer by the dancers. We arrived about eight, and it was still very quiet, only a few dancers working the stages and no one, as yet, indulging in lap dances. Eric introduced me around and then went about his business, which essentially consisted of keeping an eye on everything, anticipating trouble. He told me if he has to kick someone out of the club, a not-uncommon occurrence, he liked to do it in a way that the troublemaker felt compelled to give him a tip for doing so.

I sat down at a table with a Coke. This club, because it is not all-nude, serves alcohol. The dancers almost always wear, and retain, two pairs of panties. The top pair is very scanty, and the pair beneath those are G-strings, which consist of fabric that might add up to the size of a postage (priority mail) stamp.

One of the dancers, I'll call her "A," sat down next to me. She had a story to tell, a gripe to air. She'd been dancing for about ten years, is twenty-eight years old, and has a small child, the father of whom is in jail, doing twenty to life. She told me most of the dancers were single mothers or students. At one point five or six dancers filed past, and she counted them off: "Single mother. Single mother. Student, student. Single mother..." She told me that her breasts were made with no other help than that of God. She was proud of this. If I had to estimate, I'd say God did not make about three-quarters of the breasts I saw that night. She asked me if I knew how to tell if a woman's breasts were all natural or "augmented." I said: "Other than by touch, no." She said hold a flashlight beneath the breast in question. If the breast lights up with a kind of orange glow—"It looks like a jack o' lantern"— it's been helped. I don't recommend bringing a flashlight on first dates, however. Besides, what a woman does with her breasts is her business!

It was only about ten o'clock, and she'd already had five drinks: Red Bull and vodka. Her gripe had to do with the rules and regulations; something to do with the distance dancers must stay from patrons. When their tops are off, it must be at least six feet. A new rule was cutting into the dancer's tips. I'm sure this is not a social injustice that will arouse sympathy in most people, but, hey, strippers need to pay the rent and feed their kids just like everyone else. I asked her if she knew Eric was a hypnotist, and she did not, though she said she always felt comfortable around him, trusted him. Unusual for her, she said.

A little later, another dancer, tonight working as a cocktail waitress, who I'll call "B," sat down next to me. She told me she lives in Tijuana. "I got kicked out of San Diego." B did know Eric was a hypnotist and credited him with helping her through some hard times.

Most of the trouble with patrons at the club have to do with improper touching and disputes over money: A guy orders five lap dances and claims he only got four. With the dancers themselves, the problems are more emotional/psychological. For example, feelings of rejection are very common. Sure, the dancers are working the men, hoping they'll buy lap dances, buy drinks, and give tips. Everybody, even occasionally the customer, seems to know the dancer's flirting and attention are not real. But the feeling of rejection that the dancers feel is real. I saw this: A was dancing early in the evening, working a gay woman sitting at the edge of the stage. Von Sydow said almost half of the patrons were women, gay and straight; I would say about a third were women on the night I was there. At the moment, there was no one else watching A. She turned her back for a few moments, to shed clothing, and when she turned around, the woman was gone. I saw a noticeable look of pain on her face and a slight deflation of her posture. Happens all the time, and it hurts. B said Von Sydow's help: His counseling (which combines hypnosis, listening skills, and positive reinforcement) saved her life. B didn't have a gripe to air. She was quite chipper, in fact. She offered to buy me a lap dance, which I declined: "No thanks, ma'am, I'm on duty!"

I saw Von Sydow handle a ruckus a little later. He told me the first thing to do when up against a volatile situation is to envision a "positive outcome frame, an expectation of an outcome that it will be OK." In this case, a couple of guys walked in without paying and were refusing to do so or to leave. It was the first time I'd felt any real tension in the place. Around midnight, it was crowded now, very loud. Somehow, Von Sydow moved them toward the door without touching either. It was as if he had an invisible snowplow jutting a few feet in front of him. Once outside, his tone became more direct, he stood more erect, making it clear how massive his chest and arms were, still talking quietly, respectfully, but firmly. In another minute the two guys are standing alone, outside, looking at each other, blinking. Eric is back inside, scanning the place for improprieties.

When I asked him about the situation, he said what he did combined bouncer skills and hypnotism skills. He used hand signals, what he calls "spatial anchors" to help direct the guys outside. I don't think he got a tip from them, but he did defuse a situation that I felt was gonna blow—one of the guys, in particular, was agitated, and probably high on something in the ballpark of methamphetamine. My night at the strip club was edifying, and completely un-erotic.

I met next the other bad boy, Steve Piccus. Steve's fifty-two, almost a full generation older than Von Sydow. He and Von Sydow met about a decade ago in a San Diego bookstore and immediately bonded. Piccus acted, for a while, as Von Sydow's mentor. They're good friends now and part-time partners. Piccus has shoulder-length, graying hair, wears tinted glasses, and a leather cowboy hat. He could pass for Native American. He's Italian.

One of the things Piccus and Von Sydow do, rare but not invented by them, is called dual induction, i.e., they both hypnotize you at the same time. I was scheduled for that in a few days. First,

I wanted to know more about some of the things I heard Steve Piccus did with hypnosis. For example, in therapeutic sessions, he teaches women how to 1) orgasm on command 2) orgasm over depression 3) have better orgasms with their lovers. And when he said orgasm, he meant full-body orgasm: "Full-body orgasms move us into a state of mind called the para-sympathetic nervous system, which releases endorphins." Endorphins: The body's favorite homemade drug. If anyone ever figures out how to synthesize endorphins and smoke them, the marijuana industry (not to mention the opiate industry) is done for. Piccus told me that all fear-based emotions are embedded in adrenaline. Whatever emotions are not fear-based are embedded in endorphins. "I teach people how to achieve this endorphin state." These sessions are absolutely legit: There is never any physical contact between the therapist (Piccus) and client, no clothing is removed, etc. He told me some hypnotherapists disapprove. He remains undeterred. Later, he said: "Sex, by the way, isn't the only way to reach this state—great laughter can do it too." It looked for a while that a client consented to my being present during one of her sessions, but it was not to be so. Sometimes writers don't get to make sacrifices for their inky trade.

Piccus talks rapid fire, jumping from one hypno-related subject to another, one quote to another. He's very animated, funny, bold. He's fond of locutions such as: "Don't care what color the cat is as long as it catches the rat," and "Shaking like a dog shitting peach seeds." I asked him what he called himself. He said: "A hypno-shamanistic healer." He got a call on his cell phone while we were in his car, and he gave a client an elaborate herbal recipe for making an unguent to treat eczema.

Both Piccus and, as I mentioned, Von Sydow have studied other related healing arts: Herbalism, shamanism, Neuro-Lingustic Programming, metaphysics, story-telling, myth. Von Sydow lived in Panama for a few years as a child, and some of his most vivid memories center around his time with indigenous people there. I asked him what he'd like to be doing in five years, and he said he'd like to be in South America, studying herbal healing and shamanistic techniques.

When Piccus fetched me to take me to Von Sydow's studio for my dual induction, he first needed to pick up a lacrosse stick for his son, a sophomore at El Cajon High School. We did and went to the school's bustling main office. Someone called for Piccus's son over the intercom, and while we waited for him, Piccus chatted up the office secretaries, again doling out an herbal remedy for a complaint one of them had. Piccus has the gift of gab and some kind of weird charm: Three or four times I saw him gently grasp a strange woman (a waitress, say) by the elbows, and tell her to look into his left eye, which he said was the gateway to the soul. None of them backed off or seemed a bit offended. His son showed up and was delighted with the stick and delighted to see his dad. There was a moment of genuine warmth between them (they'd last been together at breakfast!), and they kissed each other before the kid went back to class. I remembered a somewhat opposite experience I had with my daughter when she was about his age: She instructed me to park two blocks from the school where I was picking her and some pals up after a dance. She preferred I not be seen at all. She didn't want me to scare away any boys!

Eric Von Sydow lives near the top of a very steep hill. He was waiting for us in his studio when we got there. On a table beside his computer was a set of long, steel, Freddy Krueger-like claws. He has a third career: He plays a comic book character called Wolverine at conventions. He'd recently returned from New York where he portrayed the character in a movie. I told him he's probably the only person on the planet who is a hypnotist, head of security at a strip joint, and Wolverine. He said, "Probably."

I'd told Piccus and Von Sydow my issue, and they'd prepared the appropriate metaphors, stories for my dual induction. I liked that they used metaphor and allegory. They both talked about synaesthesia, the mixing of the senses, an inherently poetic tool—to think/imagine in two or three senses distills and enriches the experience. The immortal poet, John Keats, would refer to a certain painting as feeling literally warm. Von Sydow said Mozart, while composing, was often thinking synaesthetically. Rhyme, to a degree, and onomatopoeia (words made from natural sounds, the sounds—particularly vowels—in certain words suggesting emotional or psychological states) were part of the process of making or choosing the metaphors, stories, allegories they were going to take me to, have me enter.

They put me under. Pretty much the same way Eric Kand did. I went willingly, happily. It's hard to explain what it feels like because it's familiar. But strange. I still get lost in daydreams, in books, all the time. This was similar, but deeper, I was supposed to be daydreaming, I was lying back in a chair, and I had two experienced tour guides happy to show me the sights.

They led me into a story about a garden. I won't get more specific than that because 1) it might reveal my issue 2) even though another client would get his/her own story, me telling mine might spoil the fun. They told the story alternately, one speaking, then the other, one on each side of me. Usually, Piccus spoke louder, with more intensity. Von Sydow's intonations more soothing, quieter. Sometimes they spoke at the same time, but I could hear each one of them distinctly, one in each ear. I asked them about this later. Did they deliberately do that? Most of the time, yes. Occasionally, they step on each other's lines.

At one point, they switched sides, without skipping a beat, the allegory getting deeper and more detailed as it went along. I consider myself a person with good imaginative abilities, but somehow the movie I was seeing/experiencing in my head was lighted differently than even the most vivid daydream or night dream. Colors were intense. Edges were sharper. It was multi-sensory. The metaphor/allegory itself was a bit hokey, and its ulteriority obvious, but I had no problem putting aside my critical mind and followed the story/allegory gladly. Did it make my issue disappear? No. Did it diminish it? Yes. To use a physical comparison: Say you had a heart operating at 50% of what you need, and there was a simple treatment to get it up to 89% capacity, would you do that?

They brought me up from the trance at the end of the story,

and after we talked about it a little while, they put me under again, this time standing. This time the exercise included holograms. It had a little bit less of the natural feeling than the garden journey did, and again, to describe it more fully would reveal something I don't want to reveal (and who cares anyway?) and maybe diminish the experience for another. Each time I was hypnotized I emerged refreshed and with what felt like a goofy grin on my face. After the session with Piccus and Von Sydow, I also felt a faint, pleasant tingling throughout my body. I asked about this, and one of them said: "It's the feeling after letting something go, like a snake shedding its skin." They told me I'd likely feel tired for a few days, maybe experience light flu-like symptoms, vivid dreams. Yes, to all three. Psychic toxins leaving my body.

I repeat, I'm a skeptic. Hypnotism works, at least it did for me. Either that or I got taken by three really good con men. If they were con men, I doubt they'd be wasting their talents on chump change like me. There's not even anything particularly mysterious about hypnosis and how it works. We know the mind can do miraculous things. The hypnotist (in the therapeutic sense) is a facilitator, a tour guide, a healer. Just like doctors and lawyers, some are better than others. I was hypnotized by men only (though Eric Kand estimated that 60–70% of hypnotherapists were women) and wish I'd also been hypnotized by a woman. Next time.

THE RUSSIAN POET OF SAN DIEGO

"Odessa": It doesn't sound like a particularly Russian word. Maybe Spanish, or Italian. Actually, it was named after Odysseus, the hero of Homer's (if Homer existed) great epic poem, *The Odyssey*. Any word, when it begins with an open "o" sound, immediately attracts my attention, probably because I have unusual synaptical onomatopoeic pleasure-firings in my brain. Metrically, Odessa would scan as an amphibrach, the middle syllable getting the stress. Don't worry, I'm not gonna get all prosodic on your asses. The word "Odessa" is tasty, balmy. It's also a city in the Ukraine in the former USSR, about as far south as you can get in Russia.

A port city on the legendary Black Sea, it has always been noted (after St. Petersburg and Moscow) for its writers and for its wonderful soup of cultures—Russian, Yiddish, and Ukrainian.

It's long been a center for Russian and Yiddish folklore, out of which comes the indispensable fiction writer, Isaac Babel. Here's a good piece of general wisdom and writing advice from that master: "No iron can stab the heart with such force as a period put just at the right place."

Alexander Pushkin (who died in a duel—a real dumb one—in 1837 at age thirty-seven) is one of Russia's greatest 19th-century poets. Though I think our own Walt Whitman, who published the first edition of *Leaves of Grass* at age thirty-seven in 1855, pound for pound, stanza by stanza, could go fifteen rounds with him, easy. Pushkin was exiled to Odessa for a little over a year for annoying the Czar. This happened often in Russia, well into the 20th century. A good deal of the 19th and much of the 20th century was tough for Russian writers. If it wasn't the Czar, then it was the gottdamn commies! One could be sent to the gulag for something one had written if it upset the Czar, and later, Stalin and his crew. And after that time…

I'm not going to get all Stalin on your asses either, but Stalin, unlike most paranoid dictators unencumbered by a conscience, had kind of a soft spot for writers, some of them. There's the famous story, perhaps apocryphal, very likely not, of Stalin calling up Boris Pasternak (at the time Russia's most famous writer) and asking him what he knew about the young poet Osip Mandlestam, who had written negatively of Stalin. The poem, usually given the imposed title "The Stalin Epigram" in English, didn't name Stalin directly, it wasn't published, only passed from mouth to ear to mouth (two of whom were likely spies). Here are a few lines from that poem: "the ten thick worms of his fingers/his words like measures of weight,//the huge laughing cockroaches of his top lip,/the glitter of his boot rims."

Stalin was worried about what poets were writing! I remember writing some fairly critical things about Ronald Reagan (though not by name either): Not a peep, no FBI agents following me around, I didn't even get audited by the IRS!

The story goes: Stalin wants Pasternak's opinion of Mandelstam's poetry. Calls him up at 2 A.M. Pasternak's shaking in his pajamas. Pasternak speaks highly of Mandelstam's poetry, but not too highly. He knew if he said Mandelstam was a great poet (which he was) Mandelstam was a dead man: He was still unknown enough to put a bullet in the back of his neck without raising much of a fuss. If he said he was lousy poet: Ditto, likely that night! So, Stalin gives Mandlestam a break, sends him into exile in 1932; first in Voronezh and later, to the Far East where he died, essentially, of starvation. It was only recently that the year and the place of his death was verified: 1938, Vladivostok. It was fourteen degrees below zero. Man's a problem? Kill the man. Problem solved. Stalin said something like that. Imagine Pasternak standing there holding the black phone after the line from the Kremlin goes dead. I was happy to read somewhere that as Stalin lay dying, he was terrified and kept saying he heard wolves howling, coming closer. He was, they were.

Mandelstam's wife, Nadezhda, had memorized all but a handful of his poems by the time he was first arrested, in case his manuscripts were destroyed, which they were. When asked why she didn't also memorize the handful she said: "Because he wrote them to another woman." Her two memoirs of the Stalin years, *Hope Against Hope* and *Hope Abandoned*, bear monumental witness to those times.

Anna Akhmatova is another great 20th century poet associated with Odessa. She was born there in 1889. Her first long poem, "Near the Sea," was written about Odessa. "Anna of all the Russias," she was called, reverently. She managed to avoid death or the gulag (though her son did not) during the Stalin years but suffered deprivation, constant surveillance, was unable to publish, etc. Her main crime: She wrote personal poems, love poems. It was Soviet Realism or nothing. To keep her son alive and get him out of the gulag, she forced herself to write a few poems in praise of Stalin. That was a burning pill, humiliating for her, but her readers understood.

Before I take us to San Diego, CA, USA, from Stalinist Russia, and introduce you to the poet Ilya Kaminsky, I want to tell you a little bit more about where Kaminsky was born and raised. You guessed it—Odessa. At age sixteen, in 1993, he came to America. As I said, Odessa is in the extreme south of Russia and its climate temperate. It's not exactly Palm Beach, though compared to the cold we associate with most of Russia, it's pretty close.

I asked Kaminsky about Odessa. He started by saying: "Russian literati are pretty Nazi in their snobbishness about location. For the last 200 years—pretty much the only years of full-time literary activity in the country—there were only two places where literature happened: St. Petersburg and Moscow. Moscow was the city associated with Tsvetaeva (Marina, another one of Russia's greatest poets. She hung herself during the Stalin era after years of exile, despair, hunger, and grief), Pasternak, and later Yevtushenko (Yevgeny) and Voznesensky (Andrei). St. Petersburg was the city of the old lit glory, from Pushkin and Lomonosov to Akhmatova, Blok, Mandelstam, and later Brodsky (Joseph, who came to America in the 1970s after being convicted in the Soviet Union for being a "parasite on society," i.e., he was a poet). Moscow and St. Petersburg poets could not stand each other—famously Brodsky and Yevtushenko." (Yevtushenko visited and toured America several times in the 70s and 80s and immigrated to the US in the 90s, and is on the faculty of the University of Tulsa. Brodsky, not too many years after winning the Nobel Prize in Literature in 1987, died of heart disease, a chain smoker, even after bypass surgery, to the end.) (Note: The parentheticals in this paragraph are mine.)

After mentioning these literary feuds and squawks, Kaminsky said: "But that sort of thing happens in every country." Quite right, Professor Kaminsky! My favorite American literary dust-up was when Ernest Hemingway (who was wearing pajamas at the time) punched Wallace Stevens in the face. I am also amused by the story of Hart Crane, because he was hot about something, tossing his typewriter out a second-story window because it would not write a letter in perfect Spanish (a language of which he knew about six words) to the president of Mexico.

Then, at sixteen, Kaminsky's father, Victor, and his family were granted political asylum in the US. This is how he explained it to me: "The reason my family got asylum has, to be honest, nothing to do with me. It would be silly of me to claim other people's medals. I was sixteen years old, I was dating girls, so Odessa was a place like any other for a sixteen-year-old who was discovering the streets and does not know the alternative. It was an exciting time. Yes, it was not fun, to put it mildly, to be a Jewish kid in the Ukrainian high school at that time, or now. But that is how things were then. My brother left for the USA first. He fell in love with a woman who was going to America, they love each other, they must live together, they got married. They wanted to have kids. So, they left. My father said, back then, if you want to go, go, but we are not going. And so my family stayed."

This was all matter-of-fact, and then he said something that did and did not surprise me: "My father was pretty well-to-do. He was able to bribe the Soviet police, so being Jewish was not so much of a problem in 1991. The problems began a few years later. USSR fell apart. My father had many friends, some of them from childhood, who were journalists. He was a businessman—involved in things as different as a brush factory to the filmmaking industry—but his friends were mostly writers. He had money, they didn't." (There's a common thing among writers in all countries, I thought!)

"They came to our house for parties often, he tried to help them out. It was a feeling of festival, in a way. When USSR fell apart, there was an air of freedom, and the journalists and writers were the first who thought everything is permitted, they can now write about any sort of corruption, they thought the pen can win battles, and so on. In Ukraine—more so than in Russia, although it is pretty much the same in Russia now—the old bureaucracy stayed in power, even though they changed party affiliations." I started thinking: The more things change…

He continued: "So when the journalists wrote about corruption, they were killed on the streets. It was pretty shocking. Pretty immediate. My father's good friend was Boris Derevyanko, a curious man, editor of the major newspaper in Odessa, who was also an opera theater historian. He wrote about corruption. He published a book about opera in Odessa. He was shot."

Kaminsky: "The problem for my father was that it really looks bad on paper when you are a Jewish man who has friends who write about the government and he helps them with money. Plus, being Jewish backfired then—when the state collapsed, there was no police to bribe."

There were no police to bribe! I had to keep reminding myself that I wasn't in a Kafka story. I was in Prague this summer, and it happened to be the 75th anniversary of Kafka's death. There wasn't a peep about it in the papers. I asked a senior Czech writer about this, and he explained simply, and a little sadly, that the Czech people have mixed feelings about Franz Kafka: Even though he lived in Prague most of his life (and wrote all his great books there), he wrote in German (there were hundreds of thousands of ethnic Germans in Czechoslovakia then), and he was a Jew.

Kaminsky again: "It was all in the street. That you are Jewish is written on your face, as they say in Russia: We beat you not in your passport, we beat you in your face."

I wanted to know more about his coming to America: "You asked about coming to USA—well I can only speak for myself, since my family came to a place only a few immigrants ever come to: Upstate New York. If we came to Brooklyn, we would be a different story. But in upstate New York, when our plane landed, and the cab took us to our apartment, it was snowing, it was Saturday, and there were NO PEOPLE ON THE STREETS (his emphasis). Coming from Odessa, which is pretty cosmopolitan, I honestly never before experienced the situation when you drive down the street in the broad daylight, and there is NOT A SINGLE HUMAN BEING WALKING (his emphasis). My first experience of USA was surreal. Like there is an atom bomb attack and everyone's just disappeared. It's a lonely country. Of course, I got used to it."

Sounds different than most immigrant arrival stories. His mother and his brother now live in Los Angeles. Tragically, his father died about a year after immigrating to the US. The causes were natural. If he had stayed in Odessa, the causes might not have been.

Kaminsky is tall (six three, at least) and, like many tall people, stoops a little, is a few pounds above lanky and, like many poets I know, somewhat heterodox in his attire—his teaching-day shirt tucked-in in front, untucked in back, unironed, and open three buttons over a standard white undershirt. His wife buttoned a few of the buttons for him before we left for class, and by the time we got there, they were undone again. He was oblivious to this. He has a big, slightly goofy grin, somewhat disheveled dark hair. I know a brilliant senior American poet who shaves himself in what one of my friends affectionately refers to as "the crop-rotation method." In other words, he misses whole swaths of his cheeks and chin, and always in different places. The American poet Theodore Roethke once lost a pair of his pants for several weeks. Eventually, he found them: On his desk!

Kaminsky lives with his wife, Katie Farris, a fiction writer, whom he met at one of his poetry readings. Their modest apartment, in the North Park area of San Diego, is spare and filled with light. I asked him how he and Katie met, and he said: "You will laugh, but our first conversation was about Kafka. When I read I had much accent, and not many folks at that moment could understand me. But ironically she had been studying Russian for quite some time. So, I thought: Here is a beautiful, smart woman who can actually understand what I say? A gift of the gods!" She's tall too, very slim, and lovely. She's a vegetarian and served us a delicious vegetarian lunch. I asked Kaminsky if he was a vegetarian too. He said: "Only when I eat with her." He referred to himself at one point as a "really lucky bastard" to have met her.

During my brief visit to his apartment, I failed to ask him if I could see his study. Most writers' studies are filled with books. I love looking at writers' bookshelves. Who said this: "Show me a writer's library, and I will tell you his biography"? I learned later that Kaminsky's study was in his garage, which made me regret even more not asking him.

By the time you read this, Kaminsky will be thirty-one. The teaching job I alluded to above is at San Diego State University, where he is an Assistant Professor of English and Creative Writing.

He happens to be severely hearing-impaired. He told me: "I got the momps (I'm leaving the spelling the way he wrote it because I think the word should be pronounced and spelled that way—it's more onomatopoeically accurate) when I was four. I never really think of myself as hard of hearing. Silly, but true. Why? Because I don't know the alternative, really. What does it mean to fully hear? Does anyone fully hear? What does it mean to be fully deaf? Sign language does not have a word for silence you know."

One of the highest compliments a poet can get is: He/she has a good ear. It means the rhythms, the cadences of the poetry, are strong. All great poetry is musical, and the music of each great poet is as distinct as Mozart is from Beethoven. Kaminsky's ear is terrific.

I asked Kaminsky if it was possible for him to talk about how he hears his own poems and others'. In his head? I loved his answer, and it could have only come from a real poet: "Not in the head so much as in the shoulders, legs, hands, chest, brows, ears, hair. You know. Exactly the same way you feel when you read poems that make you go nuts." The "go nuts" he is talking about is, for me, goosebumps, and, sometimes, an electric eel running up and down my spine. For people who love poetry, it's like a narcotic. Free. Though usually hidden in rare objects called books, which are sometimes hidden deep (it's a conspiracy, I tell you!) in places called bookstores and libraries.

Then Kaminsky said: "I don't think poems are heard so much as lived through. They are experiences, pieces of life on the page. Elizabeth Bishop wrote 'One Art' over twenty years ago. A crunky (again, his spelling and, I believe, more accurate for Bishop) old lady. Didn't like people much. But her poem moves my lips when I wake in the middle of the night. It tells me how to go on when I forget I should. Is that something we hear? Sure.

But it is more."

Indeed it is. Here's another thing about Kaminsky to keep in mind, particularly when you consider his hearing loss (not far from 100%), the reality of his coming to America at sixteen, and speaking little English: It seems he left a girlfriend or two behind in Odessa, and what that will do to a young man's heart does not even come close to what we usually call "broken." I have a theory: All young men's poetry begins with a broken heart. Kaminsky graduated high school, college (University of Rochester) and a prestigious (Georgetown) law school, all by the time he was twenty-four. I asked him, on a scale of one to ten, how well he spoke English when he first came to the US. He said: "When I came to US, I did not speak English. So, on a scale of one to ten, it is zero."

He practiced law for a few years in the San Francisco Bay area. I asked him about that: "Well, let me be honest. My not practicing law is no great loss for the American legal system! I worked as a law clerk for the National Immigration Law Center and after that for the Bay Area Legal Aid. It was a fantastic experience for me, in many ways. Real people, especially in the time at Legal Aid, real people, with real stories, came in hour after hour, day after day, and everyone's face had different wrinkles, and they all carried a piece of paper that somehow fucked up something in their days. It was an incredible experience being able to add a piece of paper to another and write up or speak up on someone's behalf and really see how their day was changed."

As screwy as the American legal system can be—there is certainly no duller writing on earth than legal writing—it must have seemed workable after growing up in the Soviet system. (Note: That said about the US justice system, I think I should quote Winston Churchill on democracy: "Democracy is a terrible form of government, except for all the others.") I think it was Flaubert who said something like: "Inside every lawyer is the shipwreck of a poet." Kaminsky obviously loved this work. When I heard he was a lawyer, I was pretty sure he wasn't in, say, corporate law. Good thing: They seem to have a dress code. Though he felt he could do some good as a lawyer, there were problems: "Things got a bit complicated for many public interest organizations when Arnold S. became our governor. He is a lot more liberal right now than he was a few years ago, when he just began. A lot of funds were cut, programs replaced, and so on. I got lucky—I found a teaching job within a year. Not everyone was that lucky. It pains me to think about these brilliant legal professionals who had to go home and watch TV because a certain program was cut or funds got re-directed. But that is what happened. It is better now, I imagine, politically, but a lot of programs that were changed it will take years to streamline again."

So this is how a nearly stone-deaf Ukrainian from the city of Odessa came to live in San Diego. He got his appointment at San Diego State because he's a poet and on the reputation, the strength of his first book, published when he was only twenty-eight, called, appropriately, *Dancing in Odessa*. It won the Dorset Prize and was published by Tupelo Press, one of the better independent publishers of poetry in the country. It also picked up a couple of other prizes after publication. It's an astonishingly good book, not just a good first book, or a good book by a young poet, but an astonishingly good book. Period. I could go on about why I think it so good a book, but this is not a book review. If it were, the last sentence would be: "Read this book!"

Let me give you a nutshell reiteration: Young man comes to America at sixteen. Speaks no English. He sat in his high school classes with a Russian/English dictionary, looking up words as fast as he could. He finishes high school, college, and law school, in less than a decade. Practices law for a few years. Gets a college teaching job. I bet there were 300 applications for that position. Publishes, in a language other than his mother tongue, a first-rate book of poems. And, oh, he's deaf.

I asked him about teaching and went to his class of graduate writing students at San Diego State. Before the seminar, we talked for a while on a balcony off the hallway of his classroom building. We were looking over rush hour traffic on I-8. He teaches an early-evening class because many of his students work and/or have families. Across the highway: A deep canyon and the town of La Mesa. The brush and the trees looked incredibly dry. It was a few weeks before the 2007 October fires.

I recently listened to a recording of the class. It was a diverse group, mostly younger people, but also a few older. I refer to students of mine who happen to be over thirty-five, as "full-fledged adults." I stretch the limit a bit on the age around which one is supposed to reach maturity. When I hit thirty-five, I extended my own schedule to forty-five. When I hit forty-five, I extended it to fifty-five. Now, having just turned sixty-one, I'm thinking sixty-five might be the right age for maturity. That is, after all, when the gummint starts giving you back some of the money they've been siphoning from your paycheck since your first paycheck.

I bring up age because I am almost exactly twice as old as Kaminsky. I've been teaching poetry reading and writing in colleges and universities for about thirty-five years. I've published eleven books of poetry. Most of my friends are writers and teachers of writing and literature. I've taught thousands of classes myself and been in the classroom with many of the best teachers of writing and literature in the country. Point I'm getting to: Kaminsky's class was a revelation (I've seen it all!) to me, it was a blast, it was relaxed, it was loopy. He sat in a big office chair at the head of the seminar table, swiveling this way and that, tilting back sometimes, leaning forward—he teaches with his whole body.

He'd go out on a limb about something having to do with a particular poem, and just when that branch was about to bend, he'd leap up to a higher limb, then another branch, then he'd jump to another tree! It might have seemed a little random to a civilian, but his teaching mind moved the same way the best poets' poems move: Filled with leaps and turns, surprising yet inevitable. Kaminsky would move from a Polish poet to a Greek poet to an American poet; different decades, cultures: One poetry.

He said to his students: "It's a super learning aid to listen to books talking to each other." Meaning one poet in one age, one culture, is writing about the same human business as another poet in another age, another culture. In this same context he said: "You can have a conversation with a dead writer." At one point, he had the whole class stand up and stretch, loosen up. He quoted Theodore Adorno, who said: "After the Holocaust how can there still be poetry?" And then he quoted the former US poet laureate, Mark Strand, who said: "After the Holocaust, how can there be lunch?" I think Strand was saying: After the Holocaust, we need poetry to go on, maybe more than ever. Poets like to say one thing that means another. Kaminsky mentioned William Carlos Williams' famous dictum: "No ideas but in things." I've always more or less agreed with that and argue against abstract language, though not abstract thought. Kaminsky does not agree with Williams: "All good poems have ideas." I think all good poems may not start with ideas, but all good poems end up discovering ideas, or, what might be called their themes. I don't like to use the word "idea" or "meaning" when talking about poetry. I like Frost's word for it: "Ulteriority." I want to know what's human and alive and authentic about a poem. Talking about attentiveness again, Kaminsky said: "You need to look at language like it's your lover's body." I wish I'd had teachers like him.

Given his hearing impairment and his accent, he is remarkably easy to understand, particularly after talking to him or listening to him for a few minutes. He has a rhythmic style of speaking and reading (more about that in a while), what I'd call a musical voice. He engaged his students fully in the class, asking questions, cajoling, poking, reminding them of what he'd said earlier and do they see the connection? They did. They loved and respected him.

I asked him more about teaching. After all, he was fairly new to it. He was honest: "Despite whatever they all say, teaching DOES NOT (his emphasis) have anything to do with one's own writing. (Note: I'm not sure exactly what he meant by this— probably that it didn't have a negative effect. A lot of writers who teach complain about teaching. My only response to this is: So don't teach. *Please* don't teach.) Kaminsky continued: "It is another art." I was glad to hear him say that, and it's true, that good teaching (and I don't mean only college teaching, but *all* good teaching) is an art, probably the most (and that's saying something!) undervalued art in our culture. He also said: "I like teaching because I like people, and because I LIKE TO SHARE SECRETS (emphasis mine). That struck me as absolutely true, but I'd never thought of it exactly like that. A teacher reveals secrets of the craft (I'm talking specifically now about the teaching of poetry by a poet) and also reveals that secrets, the things we discover, what we truly feel, tend to emerge when we (if we are honest) write. I love what Robert Frost said when someone asked him why he wrote poems. He said he writes "in order to find out what I didn't know I knew." I also love what Randall Jarrell said when people asked him what he wrote about. He said: "The laughter and the tears."

Kaminsky had a universal complaint made by almost all writer/teachers: "So, it is fun for me. But I also know it takes time from what I need to do most. And yet, such joy when a student gets it, the way they think of their days as changed, the ways "making" enters. (Walt Whitman said: "You say I contradict myself. Alright then, I contradict myself!") Surely, not every student will become a wonderful poet, although I have been lucky so far with students, but there is a great worth, I feel, in teaching them the 'making' of craft in itself, of attentiveness. I go with Celan (Paul, German poet) here, who said, beautifully: 'Attentiveness is the natural prayer of the human soul.' I love that."

So do I, and have quoted it to students for years although I didn't remember who originally said it until Kaminsky reminded me. I was also glad he made reference (consciously—most likely—he's read everything) to Horace, the great Latin poet, who said that poetry was a "made" thing, meaning it doesn't just happen, flow down your arm like an electric current on a direct line from Mt. Parnassus, it's not dreamy automatic keening. Kaminsky knew, though it didn't come up, that the word "poet" derives from the ancient Greek: "Maker."

He continued about teaching at San Diego State: "Well, I did not tell them, but I would do it for free. It is a luxury to talk about things you love with students. Sharing lines that can make your days brighter—what can be better?"

As I said, I earn the bulk of my living beneath the leafy shade of Academe. I've been on committees (nothing, *nothing*, is more tedious than academic committees!) making decisions regarding hiring, curriculum, tenure, etc., many times. If the people who make those decisions at San Diego State asked for it, my recommendation would be: Make sure he stays. He will be one of the best poets of his generation. He's a wonderful teacher. He will bring honor to your university. Come to my grave in thirty years or so, or to the spot where my daughter will tell you she scattered my ashes, and tell me I was right.

For years, I've ended the last class of every semester by saying something like: I wish all of you get as lucky as I have as far as finding a way to pay for a roof and to feed your child (children). Doing something you love to earn your living, I tell them, is one of the greatest blessings in life. I call them knuckleheads—by the end of a semester they know this as an endearment—and I tell them I hope they take poetry with them on their journey.

Kaminsky wasn't finished about teaching and the possibility of a greater community of writers: "I am lucky. I have wonderful, attentive students. I hope to find a way to have more of a literary community in San Diego, to bring more people together, to have more readings, conversations. If I am to stay here and live here, it would be really nice to have more of that, and I think that will happen, we will try, anyway."

I've struggled to find a few words to describe Kaminsky's overall demeanor, but I believe it comes down to something as simple as this: He is a happy man (though every happy man has his dark places), he loves his art, he loves his loved ones, he is filled with a kind of gratitude, and he loves the world—despite a million reasons not to.

Kaminsky and I were invited to give a poetry reading at D. G. Wills, a bookstore in La Jolla. It's one of the best indie bookstores on the West Coast. It's the only bookstore I've ever been in that has a street sign with several large-caliber bullet holes in it hanging on the wall. Not to mention thousands of new and used books. I'd read there several years before. Bookstores are to poets (all writers, almost all of whom are prodigious readers) what bar rooms are to rumdums. When we first walked in, Kaminsky went right to the shelves, trying to find something new. People nuts about poetry get to know the poetry shelves of the bookstores they frequent so well that they can immediately tell if something's changed—if there are new books, if books are gone, etc. Kaminsky's got that eyeball. Within minutes of entering the bookstore, Kaminsky had several books beneath his arm and was reading another with his free hand. At one point, I saw him write a note on his wrist.

It was a warm evening, a wide door in the back opened onto a small patio. To anyone who's never been to a poetry reading: There are two common stereotypes—1) it will include finger snapping and bongos or 2) a boring old guy will mumble incomprehensible poems incomprehensively into a page in front of an audience in deep pain, especially for the man who was forced by his wife to go to the reading. The former hardly ever happens anymore, the latter, unfortunately, still happens sometimes. But: Pretty frequently, poetry readings are lively affairs: Funny, rapid, sexy (this gets the attention of students), and intensely alive. Concerts without instrumentation.

Although I realize it is a somewhat sexist thing to say, I tell my young male students at Georgia Tech, as a way of getting them to go to poetry readings we hold on campus: "Chicks dig poetry. The readings are free. She might think you're *sensitive*." One of my best students at Georgia Tech is also one of the top college linebackers in the country. He'll be drafted this spring and be in the NFL next fall. Another student once told me he wanted to be in my class because there were more girls in it than in most classes at Tech. I told him to pass that news around and then let him in the class for his honesty. If I can get them to the water, some of them turn out to be thirsty.

Once in a while I'll get a student a little on the macho side, with a poetry-is-for-girls attitude. I ask him if he'd have the guts to write the aforementioned poem that Mandlestam wrote regarding Stalin. Backs the dude right up. That doesn't work? I get my linebacker guy to have a little chat with him. I got a call recently from a former female student at Tech—she just married a guy she'd met in one of my classes. He isn't good enough for her (my daughter is about her age; no guy's good enough), but poetry brought them together. A former student of mine, now a widely-published poet, fell in love with another poet at my house at a party after a poetry reading. Their second child was born recently. I have lots more anecdotal evidence of the aphrodisiacal properties of poetry. Gentlemen?

I loved hearing Kaminsky read. He passes out copies of his poems for the audience to follow along as he reads them aloud. I had heard his reading style described as operatic, and I guess it is, but it is really impassioned speech, very much in the Russian tradition of declaiming one's poetry, emphatically. Not theater, not oral interpretation, but excited, intense human speech—he would raise and lower his voice, change his pacing. His voice has the faint, joyous echo of bells tolling.

Poetry has been around at least as long as the cave paintings. Poetry existed before language: The first poets were primitive people dancing around a fire and chanting rhythmically. Their themes were probably the next day's hunt, or their spirit world. Every culture on earth developed poetry on its own, independent of other cultures. Like fire. Like the spear. We've always known, because our bodies told us so, that we derive pleasure from the repetition, and the variations of repetition, of certain sounds: Music, poetry. Now we know that it is a truly physiological human need, or source of pleasure: CAT scan machines can record the brain's pleasure centers lighting up when listening to music or the cadences of poetry.

Russians particularly love their poetry and their poets. Always have. If you meet a Russian diplomat, or student, or waiter, or, especially, a Russian cab driver, ask him or her to recite some favorite poems. I once got a free, rather lengthy ride, from a Russian cabbie because he was so delighted that I knew (in English only) many of the Russian poets. Russians say that people who love to read and write poetry have "Nightingale Fever." Before the fall of Communism, it was not unusual for poets to draw almost stadium-sized audiences for readings. For poets who were deemed unacceptable to the regime (if they were not exiled, or jailed, or put in phony laughing academies), there were smaller, but no less intense, private gatherings. There was a form of publishing called *samizdat*, i.e., manuscripts passed hand-to-hand by readers.

Truly American and truly Russian literature began about the same time, give or take. American poets, until Whitman and Dickinson, were really English poets, American poets writing after the English model and in the English tradition, which was only natural. But after we'd been around for a while, we started minting our own American English. See Whitman, who, one critic said, established "an absolute discontinuation of the traditions of English verse," and Dickinson, above. Kaminsky had this to say about Russian poetry in the 19th century: "Russian literary life… did not begin until the 1820s (OK, so the Russkies were a few decades ahead of us in developing their national literature—we beat them to the moon!) when Pushkin was writing his great *Eugenie Onegin*, Gogol was beginning to write, and in a few years, Lermontov. Pushkin wrote in Russian—not the French language of nobility." We agreed, generally, on this parallel, but he also reminded me that American poets had, via our literary ancestors, Shakespeare, about whom Emily Dickinson said: "Why do we need anything else?" Kaminsky said Russian poets did not have a Shakespeare. He referred to Shakespeare's work as our "epic." Hard to argue. For Russian literature, this had a good side though: "That absence of the great literary past in the Russian language does explain, to my mind anyway, the abundance of the epic novels—Tolstoy, Dostoevsky—in the late 19th century." The gods of literature giveth and they taketh.

Joseph Brodsky was said to have been asked, after he came to America, what was worse—living in a society where you could be sent to the gulag for writing something that displeased the bosses, or living in a society where a writer can write anything he or she wants, as critical of the bosses as he or she wants, and nobody cares? He said the former. I'm not sure I believe him. First of all, some people do care. And, second, he seemed pretty happy in the US. He picked up a half-million dollar MacArthur grant. I once saw him drive away from a poetry reading in a BMW.

A former student of mine, who teaches at a San Diego high school, brought a bunch of his students to the reading at the bookstore. Afterwards, some of the kids wanted us to sign their arms. Not something I've ever been asked to do before. I wrote on one skinny arm: "Give this kid an A!"

Kaminsky signed a few too, in English, American English, because that is the language he writes in now. Stanley Kunitz, the great and beloved American poet, who died at age 100 just a few years ago, said of himself, and of other poets: "I have a tribe, but we are scattered." Yes, true, but we sometimes gather in small groups of two or three, sometimes in much larger confabs. See the annual Dodge Poetry Festival in New Jersey (15,000 over a weekend), see the Associated Writing Program's yearly convention this winter in NYC: 7,500 (c'mon, that's too many; no, that's not enough!) writers.

It's not writers that are important. What's important is the writing, the poems, stories, plays, novels, etc. Immensely important. One of the last things Kaminsky said to me was: "And, about poetry, I am not sure if I had said it before, so I want to say it now—I want to make sure it is clear how joyous the activity of writing is, how wondrous, magical. I don't want the biographical or historical to cloud that up. Writers' biography/history, after all, is in their language."

If you get a chance to read Ilya Kaminsky's poems, or hear him read, do so. His poems will make you feel a little more alive and a little less alone. And if you happen to see him on the street, most likely he will be the best poet you ever see on the street.

3 A.M.

There is no night anymore. In or around cities, in suburbs and small towns, there is no night. It still gets dark, and the days still get longer or shorter. Lights are everywhere—large, harsh, powerful, all pushing back the dark.

Not much more than a hundred years ago, the only things lighted were lighted by fire. There was something about these hours—three to four—in the morning that I had forgotten: A romance, a dread, solitude, an atmosphere, and a tone.

For many years I lived as an almost completely nocturnal person. I would stay up until the first peeps of dawn. Then I'd sleep until noon or one. I have a friend who still makes fun of me about the time he called at noon, and I yelled at him for calling so early. I liked to write, I liked to walk, particularly in NYC; I liked to read. Reading alone at night: Perfect. Wallace Stevens has a poem with these lines: "The house was quiet and the world was calm./The reader became the book; and summer night/Was like the conscious being of the book./The house was quiet and the world was calm." I liked that the phone didn't ring, there was little traffic, I liked being awake when most others were asleep.

The best time-clock job I ever had was as a night watchman at a small women's college in Cambridge, MA. I got to work about six, had a free meal in the college cafeteria, walked around the campus and turned on lights, and read a lot in old armchairs, which the buildings-and-grounds day-crew used to duck into and goldbrick. These were set up around the boilers in the basements of classrooms and dormitories, especially good places to read in the colder months. I think I only made about seventy-five bucks a week (it was 1971), but I probably got to read three or four books a week on the job. I considered that a serious perk. This job also provided me with another free meal later and all the toilet paper and light bulbs I needed: I was the night watchman, I had the keys to everything. There was another watchman on the same shift. He was about eighty years old. His name was Tom too. I was in my early twenties. They called us Old Tom and Young Tom, in the same sense as you'd call people Frick and Frack or Tweedledum and Tweedledee. It is a blazing miracle that no serious trouble occurred on our shift. We had the keys, and we turned on some lights, but we did not own the night.

For most of my life, however, I've made my living as a college teacher, an even better racket than the night watchman deal, and arranged my classes for afternoons or evenings. My nocturnal ways were changed, I think forever, about fifteen years ago. Fatherhood. The only time to sleep was when the baby slept, and my daughter seemed to sleep little. And she was an early riser. I'll never forget my pleasure the first time—she was about ten—when I got to wake her up. I poked her leg and said the thing I hated to hear when my parents woke me up as a child: "Rise and shine." A parent's revenge may be slow in coming, but it is sweet.

Now I love mornings, the light hours of which I rarely saw for so many years. I wanted to try to change that circadian clock again, if only for a week or so. We really do carry clocks around in us in the form of a tiny clump of cells known as the suprachiasmatic (nice word in which you hear other words) nucleus, or SCN. This clock is highly sensitive to the daily change from light to dark, with the rising sun setting us up for wakefulness, and the dusk setting us up for sleep. We're programmed by these circadian rhythms to sleep at night and be awake during the day. I'd try to flip the switch. I wanted to know what was out there in the night. Who might know about the night, the darkness, literal and figurative? The cops. They do their best business at night.

I went out on a 9 P.M. to 7 A.M. (he works a ten-hour shift four days a week) ride-along with a young (twenty-six), smart, tough, aggressive cop from the Chula Vista PD named Scott Schneider. He's about six three, maybe 200 pounds and, like so many young cops today, ripped. He works out, lifts weights just about every day. It relieves stress and "helps if I have to fight guys." He wears a bulletproof vest and over that another smaller vest, about the size of a dinner plate, right in the middle of his chest. He keeps a small handgun tucked in there, carries a regulation weapon on his hip, and another, smaller caliber gun strapped to his ankle. He also carries a knife. I didn't ask where.

He's a graduate (a BA in English with a minor in Creative Writing) of San Diego State, where he played three years of varsity basketball. He's in his second year on the force. I liked him right away. I always respect cops and usually like them. Even in the 60s, as a card-carrying hippie and a half-assed radical, I was never comfortable with "the cops are the pigs" attitude. To me that was like making an enemy out of teachers or farmers, people who do work that has to be done and done well if we are to survive as a civilization. Plus, cops' work is dangerous. Every day a cop thinks about the department's chaplain walking up his sidewalk to ring his doorbell and tell his wife, or father, or mother that something bad has happened. So: If you're going to badmouth cops, don't do it around me. I know lots of young men about Scott Schneider's age. Most of them are graduate students, studying the writing and reading of poetry. I hope Officer Schneider applies someday what he learned as a creative writing student in college—he'll have something to write about.

I asked Schneider what happens out here at three, four in the morning. He said: "People get arrested." And a very common thing to get arrested for nowadays is methamphetamine. Since crystal meth can keep people awake for two or three nights in a row, not to mention agitated and paranoid, it's not uncommon for meth users to cross paths with the cops. He said he hardly ever sees other drugs, rarely cocaine or crack, infrequently heroin. Cops don't bother with small amounts of marijuana, but if they find it on you while frisking you, and they find nothing else and kick you loose, they make you dump it out on the street—probably more painful to a dedicated pothead than a ticket or even an arrest.

I was wondering if there was a pie chart (I love pie charts!) somewhere that estimated what percentage of people were awake through the night because of controlled substance consumption, plain old insomnia, jobs, night terrors, other. I think it was in the "other" category that I used to live my nocturnal life.

We cruised around Chula. He has a more-or-less regular area to cover that he can leave in an instant if he gets a call. He follows his nose, and his instincts, around. He glanced down a side street and saw a car stopped, lights off, in the road. Why? Drug deal, a hooker? He checks it out. It's a woman he's busted before. This time there's no bad business going on.

A little later he notices an old Cadillac pulling into a convenience store. Two males, one white, one African-American. He waits for them to come out, then follows them to a light, where they fail to come to a full stop before taking a right. He pulls them over. They said they'd driven the several miles from San Diego to Chula to this convenience store to get a Popsicle. Officer Schneider said: "They don't have any 7-Elevens in San Diego?" He invites the driver, the black man, to step out, and asks if he can search him. He consents. There was a local TV clown where I grew up who would pull a huge number of things, including dozens of bananas, from his trick suit. His name was The Banana Man, natch. That was his whole act. I thought this guy was auditioning for the part. Schneider held the man's laced-together fingers behind the man's back with his right hand and went through his pockets with his left. Onto the trunk of the car went one white lace-topped woman's sock, a soda can, three or four packs of cigarettes in various stages of depletion and a couple of brands, a pin for a bicycle pump, two or three disposable cigarette lighters, a few pencils, a long woman's nylon stocking, a candy bar, napkins, change, an empty plastic bag not much bigger than a postage stamp (who makes sandwiches this small?) with slight white powder residue—not enough.

Schneider told me later he thought the guy was clean as he searched him: Most often, particularly if the officer is getting close, the person being searched squeezes the cop's hand holding his fingers behind his back. It's as if by squeezing this hand, it will stop the officer's other hand from finding the dope or weapon. It's a kind of involuntary body language, a "tell," a tactile sign. The cops call the watch pocket of jeans "the bingo pocket"—always a good chance you'll find a few rocks in there. This guy didn't squeeze Schneider's hand. Officer Schneider told the white guy to take a seat on the curb. Schneider kind of half-heartedly searched him and then the car. He found a small bag of pot underneath the passenger seat. Schneider had seen the guy ditch it there when he pulled them over. He dumped the pot on the street. The white guy was just finishing up an ice cream cone. He looked a little sad. Officer Schneider seemed to take no joy in this.

At another stop later, a backup cruiser arrived with two officers. In Chula, officers ride alone, but backup units arrive with great alacrity. It took me a few minutes to recognize one of the officers: Steve Fobes, an agent in the Family Protection Unit at CVPD. I didn't recognize him right away because he was in uniform, and when I hung around with him a bit last year, he always wore plainclothes. He was riding as a "ghost": A more experienced cop who rides along with a new cop. It's one of the last phases of police training. He doesn't advise or even speak a word to the young cop he's going around with—he's a silent, ghost observer. He then evaluates the young cop's job. He could talk to me, though, and we did a little. It was almost exactly 3 A.M. He mentioned that he'd arrested a guy he was looking for intensely a year ago, a particularly nasty pedophile. He told me then and I quoted him then: "It's only a matter of time until we get him." So it should be said here, in print: He and his colleagues made good that promise.

We talked on the corner of Broadway and C Street, a clean, well-lighted place. Streetlights are fairly recent—if you don't count bonfires at crossroads in ancient Athens. It wasn't until late in the 17th century, in Paris, where a priest with an eye for a franc obtained a monopoly on lighted watch posts. They were 300 paces apart. You could hire a guard with a lantern to escort you from one to another. The abbot did pretty well for himself, taking a cue from God when He said, "Let there be light."

About 3:15, a Code 3 came over the radio, and soon we were pushing 125 mph on 5 North. It's a very rare call and means, essentially: Everybody get there fast. It's used when shots are fired or an officer is down. We were the second unit there, and Steve jumped out to help with the arrest. A guy was getting cuffed. It was on the edge of an empty lot next to warehouses. There was light everywhere—from the buildings, streetlights, parking lot lights, and soon, a half dozen cop cars. Yep, people get arrested at 3 A.M. You'd be amazed at how little time it takes a whole lot of cops to get to a scene after this kind of call. Steve was pumped by the ride and the brief struggle. The guy was an escapee, I believe. It was one of the few Code 3s Steve's been on. I imagine there must be, potentially, many adrenaline-pumping moments in any given night (or day) on the job for a cop. Nightshift workers, in general, have more sleep problems than dayshift workers. Officer Schneider said he had sleep difficulties—insomnia—frequently. Nightshift workers also have more gastrointestinal problems than dayshift workers. They tend to eat poorly. I didn't ask Officer Schneider if he had stomach problems or ate too much junk food, but if a cop already has the common nightshift problems, and their job also has the potential to get them shot—those cops might have an even tougher time of it.

Another part of the 3 A.M. contingent would be regular old insomniacs. They're not usually out on the street, however. The reasons for their sleeplessness? There are a million stories in the naked city. You know these wakeful only by the light of one window here, one window there, in a cityscape of a million dark windows. I have been a member of these Morpheus-deprived. I used to worry about it sometimes. Which, of course, made it worse. Then somebody told me, you'll fall asleep when you're tired enough. Turned out to be true. Sometimes, you just need to stay awake until you fall asleep. I've always loved Robert Frost's poem of the sleepless, "Acquainted with the Night." The first two stanzas go like this: "I have been one acquainted with the night. /I have walked out in rain—and back in rain./I have out-walked the furthest city light.//I have looked down the saddest city lane. /I have passed by the watchman on his beat/And dropped my eyes, unwilling to explain." It is possible to out-walk the furthest city light—go to the desert, the mountains, the sea—but the lights are everywhere here.

I watch dawn begin to arrive in the parking lot of a Motel 6. Officer Schneider had said, about 4 A.M., "Let's go the Motel 6 parking lot and throw somebody in jail." We'd cruised through a few times earlier. He's found several stolen cars here. He needed to find one more stolen car to reach a certain number, and he'd get a pin to wear on his uniform. A humble reward, but a matter of pride: He wanted one more car. He liked finding stolen cars—the results were tangible and almost immediate: Somebody got their car back. He noticed a Toyota with a sorority sticker on it. "What would a sorority girl be doing in a place like this?" He ran the plates. Not this time.

He'd questioned a guy earlier in the parking lot, and the guy left. Now his jeep was back. The guy was in a room but not registered. Officer Schneider's nose was telling him: Dope deal. A few backups arrive. They try a "knock and talk": They don't have a warrant or any probable cause to toss the room, so they knock, and when the guy finally comes to the door, another officer, who has a knack for talking his way into places, speaks to the guy. No luck. The guys inside are too savvy, and even though the cops saw a knife and a black metal box, they couldn't go in. They were getting a little frustrated. It was a standoff. Schneider and the other cops discussed what to do. Traffic was picking up on 5 going both North and South. A eucalyptus tree was rattling in a slight breeze. From the worn-down dirt, among crushed beer cans and cigarette butts, a few very delicate and very yellow little flowers poked out from cracks in the asphalt. Even a little light grew from the ground. The parking lot's lights buzzed. Things happen at this hour of the morning or night: Harsh knocks on motel room doors; tired, frustrated cops. The guy came out of the room, got in his jeep. Keeping on his case, they give him a sobriety test, which he passed.

They sent him on his way. He was a scraggly dude but very cool—patient, cooperative, and slightly condescending. He smirked as he got back in his ride. He'd be making his dope deal later. The light went off in the motel room. Scott said, "Let's go look for stolen cars." He knew a place where the chances were good.

I always liked Allen Ginsberg's poem "A Supermarket in California." He calls it the "neon fruit supermarket" and writes of "peaches and penumbras." I never liked much else of his except for *Howl* and chunks of "Kaddish." It seemed to me he was too much into the guru business the last three or four decades of his writing life. Gurus have the answers, are happy to tell you the path. Gurus hold too much light. Guru-ism isn't good for poets. As I said, I've never been a huge fan of his work, but after reading a recent biography, it was clear that he was a kind and generous man.

I thought it would be fun to find and visit the toniest 24-hour supermarket in San Diego. It shall remain unnamed. Who goes shopping at 3–4 A.M., and what do they buy? How many different kinds of smoked oysters does the place stock? I've always used the Smoked Oyster Index to judge the fussbudget food market. I try not to imagine how oysters get smoked: Do they hang them in a smoke house, individually, like hams? In or out of their shells?

The first thing that struck me about this store was how much booze was for sale. Where I'm from (New York) you can only buy beer or wine in a supermarket, never distilled spirits. Incredible arrays of wines and beers and the hard stuff here. Somebody once told me that booze was about a third of the profit a restaurant makes. Is booze then a third of our regular food budget?

I never saw so much candy in my life, including about eighty different kinds of gummy bears, all of which are particularly useful for removing fillings: cola bottles, octopus, DH Sharks,

Gummi Twin Cherries, Sour Patch Fruit salad... The possibility of a stroke not withstanding, I am glad I have a salt-tooth rather than a sweet-tooth. Every olive oil on the planet was there, not to mention cheeses from the milk of 10,000 cows, goats, and buffaloes. Look up Donald Hall's wonderful poem "O Cheeses"— it's a different kind of treat for the mouth, as well as a pleasure for the ear.

It was about 3:30 A.M. Who was shopping here? Exactly three other people. Two gay men were selecting a large number of oranges, each one becoming more orange as they lifted it to the light to inspect it. A punked-out young woman with a large tattoo, UNJOY, in gothic script across her upper back, was buying a six-pack of soda. The reference to UNCOLA is certainly conscious, a kind of ironic, albeit permanent, comment on American consumerism. There're lots of reasons to satirize the excesses of capitalism, but usually satire puts the needle to the subject rather than the needle being put to the satirist.

I had time to ponder this: I was on a mission to fruits and vegetables. The orchard/garden of the world! Sometimes writers write things (especially if they're not getting paid, as in poetry, for example) as an excuse to use certain words. Just because they like the word's sound, taste, connotations. For example: Graffiti eggplant, red camarillo, sweet lemon (oxymoronic fruit!), red banana, baby pineapple, burro bananas (they carry the red bananas on their backs), malanga. I'm not sure I'd want to eat any of these, but they are tasty words! The lettuce section had many shades of green and mists and even occasional artificial thunder. I closed my eyes and was compelled to lean over the bins—until I started getting damp. There were yellow peppers bright enough to act as nite-lites. And, Lordy, Lordy, the carrots so bright in their orange and their wild, green hair. I considered never eating a pork chop again! There was one little green pepper on which I did some research. It is grown exclusively in the magma chamber of a volcano in Mexico. Alas, I didn't see anyone who looked like Walt Whitman or García Lorca squeezing melons and eyeballing the bag boys, as Ginsberg did. The store was blazing bright, brighter than in full daylight. You had to look hard to find a shadow.

I wandered up and down the aisles, lonely, eavesdropping on the conversations of stock-boys: They were talking about Gameboys. The night manager gave me a tour (which he wasn't supposed to do, which is why the store is not named) of the storerooms, the meat locker, and, let's call it, the fish locker. He had the most bloodshot eyes I've ever seen. This was one of his three jobs, one for each of his children, he joked. Night-workers average less sleep during the workweek than dayshift workers. All the extra work people do—odd hours, evenings, weekends, round-the-clocks—has reduced American sleep time by 20% this century. A hundred years ago people slept, on average, 1/5 more. Which means they dreamed more.

Which means they probably experienced hypnagogia more frequently. Coleridge mentions hypnagogia in his notebooks: "The whispers just as you have fallen or are falling asleep—what are they and whence?" Indeed. Especially, "whence?"

There was less to do after dark when Coleridge wrote his note. There were many fewer lights. You had to spend a lot of time hitching and unhitching horses. And even more time cleaning up or avoiding their road apples.

When we went backstage at the supermarket, I saw a wooden pallet piled fifteen feet high with cases of Diet Coke. The store sells 180 twelve-packs of Diet Coke a day. That's over 2,000 cans of Diet Coke a day and not a single calorie! They must weigh about eight tons but not a single calorie! It's a freaking miracle! And it's just right for washing down gummy bears and, oh, seventeen kinds of smoked oysters. I stuck my head in the meat locker and in the fish locker: Lots of meat, lots of fish.

What are babies doing at 3 A.M.? I know a lot of people without babies are thinking that. As I said, mine was often awake. My job at 3 A.M. was to get our daughter from her crib in the next room and bring her to my wife, who would nurse her; then, when they both were conked out again, take our daughter back to her crib. I could do it in my sleep. I did. This is part of new fatherhood: You carry the baby sometimes, the rest of the time you carry stuff for the baby that weighs about fifty times more than the baby.

I found a sleeping baby. She was a friend's baby. He easily agreed to let me sit in his baby's room for a few hours in the middle of the night and "take down my impressions." His wife thought I was crazy but consented. There was a delay in her consent, however, during which time, I believe, she had me checked out by the FBI. The baby, Nina, six-months-old, slept on her back, her arms and legs bent and cocked. She pedaled the air every once in a while—her dreams were telling her she'd be running someday. Her crib was stuffed with stuffies. Outside her bedroom window, a lemon tree scraped against the house. An outside light glinting off the lemons made them shine like Christmas ornaments. I could make out some books on the shelves—some poetry, some biographies of poets. Her father is a poet and a public school teacher. This means she's going to grow up poor and deeply loved. She is unconcerned about that now. There was one light on in the room—in her crib, a little green glowing bead: The baby monitor. She snuffled a little.

I leaned over and sniffed her head. I love to sniff babies' heads. Until recently, I thought if this was not quite a perversion, then at least I was a little weird. And as far as I know there are no Twelve-Step groups for people powerless over sniffing babies' heads. It turns out (this is scientific fact!) a baby's head and hair contain an endorphin or an enzyme, or something like that, which adults find pleasurable. That's right: You get a little buzz from sniffing a baby's head. I imagine it came to be as a way for a baby to help ensure adult care and love. I predict this: Pretty soon we'll begin seeing ads in the back of magazines for a men's hair product that includes these chemicals. Men will do anything to lay their heads on a woman's heart.

Meanwhile, not much was happening with this baby. She was pretty bald and no new hair sprouted. Her calves were chubby and pink. A few unpleasant looks passed over her face: Dreams or gas? I remembered one 3 or 4 A.M. when my child was feeling poorly and I just had all my wisdom teeth pulled. Since neither of us could sleep and both of us were fussy, I took her downstairs and lay with her on my chest on the couch, and pretty soon she was asleep, and the pain in my jaw was gone. Thank you, sweet Nina, for helping me remember that. I have this advice for your father: Stop time, stop time right now! So this is another thing that happens at 3 A.M.: A baby sleeps oblivious (as she should be) to the sadness of the world. Far in the distance, I heard a police siren.

What happens if your parakeet has a seizure in the middle of the night? You take him to an all-night pet hospital. And, if you're lucky, you'll take beloved Tweety to the hospital where Dr. Barrie Sands works. She's petite, brown-haired, attractive, and originally from upstate New York. She's got the touch not many human doctors seem to have nowadays: She listens to her patients, she's got what you call good bedside manner. Her patients can't talk, of course, but they still need listening to, and sometimes the owners need more care, and certainly more assurance, than the pet.

She told me once, when she was a young vet, a woman came to her office cradling an invisible dog in her arms. The dog was sick, and she loved it and wanted a vet to save it. Dr. Sands took the invisible dog from the woman's arms, laid him on a table, pretended to examine him, declared him 100% healthy, handed him gently back to his relieved and grateful owner. No charge. I wanted to kiss her when she told me that story.

She gave me a tour of the ward. There was a big, forlorn-looking dog with most of the hair on his back shaved off and a lengthy, stitched incision running along his spine. Vertebrae problems, he's doing well. I have a friend with vertebrae problems—he's not doing OK. He has so much pain he can barely walk a block without tears coming to his eyes. Dogs and cats have bum backs, kidney problems, get cancer and chemo. I neglected to ask if all of their fur falls off.

There was a cockatiel back here who had a run-in with a window fan. It ripped a lot of his feathers off and some new ones—they're called blood feathers—were growing in. A dog without fur looks bad enough, a bird missing most of its feathers is a very sorry-assed looking creature.

Since this was an emergency ward, I wanted to know, naturally, what kind of emergencies reptiles have. Fact is: They have few. She did treat a snake once that had been duct-taped to a pole. The owner's version of a leash or a chain? There was another snake that got into a neighbor's yard and the neighbor took a hammer to it.

Dogs and cats have traumas, emergencies: Hit by cars and, a growing problem, coyotes. They have flat-out heart attacks. She's seeing a lot of ferrets lately. Ferrets were popular pets for a while. I had a student who brought one to class a few times—it would dash around the room right along the baseboards and then climb up into her lap. It was a nervous creature, but poetry seemed to calm it, or bored it into a stupor. Dr. Sands has done operations on goldfish. She referred to the animals as patients. She kept using words—lymphoma, remission, infarction, etc.—that you expect to hear only when talking about human illness, but as I said: Animals get cancer, they have heart attacks, and bum backs, and sore feet. She likened her work to a pediatrician's: Babies and small children can't say where they hurt or what's wrong with them either.

We went from bed to bed. Actually from cage to cage— but "cage" does not seem like the right word. There was a tiny shivering Chihuahua suffering from seizures. I've never liked little yappy dogs. I was tempted to ask how one can tell these ever-trembling creatures are having a seizure, but that would have been rude to this kind doctor, and I also got the feeling, in a flash, that if I made a wiseacre comment, I'd get bit by a dog the second I walked out on the street. A big, dopey-looking mongrel, who'd had chest surgery for cancer, lost three ribs, and one lung, was hanging in. Somebody loves him. She mentioned the next-of-kin's—the owners'—right to refuse euthanasia. People will do just about anything to buy a little more time for a pet. I once watched my father drown a litter of barn cats. He put them in a burlap sack and then in a bucket of water. It was a necessity. They were so young they weren't even cute yet. Still, it tore him up.

I spent a few hours at the pet hospital. No new emergencies

came in. Dr. Barrie said this was unusual. When I walked out to the parking lot about 5 A.M., a rabbit hopped across my path. And when I turned on the car lights, a huge spider web spanned a parking barrier. The web hadn't been there when I arrived. This creature had been busy, and I lingered a few minutes in the running car, lights on, hoping to attract a few moths for its breakfast.

I thought that going to a cemetery at 3 A.M. might be a good idea. I scouted a pretty isolated one, access to which seemed easy. I arrived, in a cab, at 3:05 A.M. on an August night. I asked the driver to wait. I told him I had to say goodbye to someone very important to me. I walked into the cemetery about fifty feet, then turned around and came out. Not because I was scared, but for two reasons: There clearly wasn't anything happening here, and it was an idiotic and disrespectful idea.

I went to an all-night gym. The night manager wouldn't let me look around. Everything was so silver and light, the dumbbells gleaming, all in a row. I wondered if that was someone's job: To polish the dumbbells. Wouldn't look too impressive on a résumé: Dumbbell polisher. An exquisitely coifed woman did crunches on an incline bench. Her hair didn't move. In the lounge, a good-looking Asian man in his twenties was massaging the neck of a beautiful woman about twenty years older. She wore a belly shirt that showed off her washboard abs. They had a combined body fat of 1%. They weren't wearing workout clothes.

I asked the manager if he knew what Mark Twain said when someone asked him about physical exercise. The manager said no. I said Twain said his bicep muscle felt like a shucked oyster in a sock. The manager kicked me out.

I walked to an all-night check-cashing place. I didn't have a check to cash, the light was blinding, and the manager here, too, eyed me warily, was uninterested in engaging in conversation.

I went into an all-night drugstore across the street. I put on a pair of sunglasses—too much light everywhere. The counter person seemed bored rather than suspicious. When I walked into places like this with a cop, people were generally friendlier. Why was that?

On another night, one of my last stops was a 24-hour diner. I'd been there several times during the day. It's a well-known place in Coronado and often the last stop for young service members after a night on the town. There were a couple of sailors in their cups eating huge quantities of eggs and potatoes and bacon. I talked to the counter man after they (half-bagged as they were, they were not in the least rowdy) left. The counter man owns a boat on which he lives. He travels up and down the coast, and when he runs out of money, he gets a cooking job for a few months, saves some money, quits, and goes back to his boat and his travels. Nice way to live I thought. His boat was at the marina near the San Diego-Coronado Bay Bridge. Must be nice to sit on deck at 3 A.M. and look at the bridge, the beautiful blue-black (at this time) bridge. I ordered a few scrambled eggs, ate them, and stumbled home, my nightshift's over.

The night's not what it's cracked up to be. I avoided clubs and bars purposefully—obvious places where nightlife happens. As I keep harping on: There's too much light everywhere. Night is a good time to hose down your sidewalk, and the traffic's minimal, but there is too much light everywhere. A sociologist named Murray Melbin says that the night was the last frontier, and since the invention of electric lighting, we have colonized night much in the same way that we colonized the Old West. He also says that time is like space: The more people occupy day and the more crowded it becomes, the more people are pushed into the night. Soon they'll be the same, one will blend into the other, and it'll be difficult to tell the difference. Or better: Maybe each day will be like René Magritte's famous surrealist painting: A daytime sky over a nighttime street. Or is it a nighttime sky in a daytime street?

WE WEEP FOR OUR STRANGENESS

I've seen my father cry once. He's eighty-five years old. I'm fifty-three. It was a little over thirty years ago; when he was about the age I am now. We were crossing the street in front of O'Brien's Funeral Home, the family funeral home, whose undertakers waked and buried everyone in my family for as long as I can remember, and before. How families choose their local funeral home and why it never changes, generation after generation—this is lost in the mists of time.

We were leaving the wake of his mother, my grandmother, who died at eighty-nine, in her sleep, with no illness beforehand. We walked across Clark Street—I remember stepping over the road's white line—and my father broke into two or three quick, wrenching sobs, and said, "She was such a good woman!" Before reaching the other side of the road, he had stopped. The next day, at the cemetery, I noticed the gravestone of an old auntie. Two letters of her last name were transposed. My father wasn't crying. I believe I did cry at the gravesite. It wasn't until later, maybe years later, I laughed about that eternal indignity: A typo on a tombstone.

She *was* a good woman—perpetually cheerful, deaf, affectionate, and speaking little English. Her deafness became total when she was about sixteen and only a few years off the boat from Germany. She could speak, therefore, despite her deafness, and did so volubly, in a kind of English/German patois. She is the only person in my life who I can say was happy to see me every time she saw me.

It's not that my father is a cold man. He isn't. First take into account: His people were German. Let's face stereotypes: Germans aren't known for their weepiness, their emotional excesses, or tenderness. Particularly German men. Italian men, for example, are capable, and culturally allowed, to be openly emotional. But my father is a gentle man who rarely raised his voice nor ever struck me as a child. Once, he kicked me in the ass, with the side of his foot, and this expression of anger astonished me. Couldn't blame him: I had put antifreeze where the oil should go, and the oil where antifreeze should go, in his car. He spent most of his working life driving a white truck around a small town and leaving bottles of milk on people's doorsteps and back porches. He was a soft touch—kids coming around his milk truck in summer and begging for a chunk of ice always got it. A few times I remember him donating an old suit for an indigent pal or the town drunk to be buried in (the wake always at O'Brien's; in a town of at least three or four funeral homes, I don't believe I ever entered another). I heard him say a bad word about only one man in my entire life: Benny the Bum. He just didn't like (because he didn't work) Benny the Bum, a part-time bookmaker and younger brother of our town's primary bookmaker, Luigi. Luigi he liked and played the same number nearly every day with him for fifty cents or a buck when he delivered a few quarts of milk to Luigi's candy store, which really was a candy store, as well as a front for his bookmaking operation. My father was/is a gentle man. As a child I suffered from crushing migraines, what we called "sick headaches." Driven home from school enough times by the nurse, I learned to throw up in my lunch box and not all over the front seat of her car. My father would enter the darkened room where I was lying with a cold cloth on my head. He'd put his hand on my forehead. His hands are very large and soft (still). He'd say: "I wish I could take the pain out of your head and into mine." He meant it. I say the same thing to my own kid, who is also prone to headaches. I've heard him say the same thing to her. But he doesn't cry. It's hard for him to hug me. He can hug his granddaughter, is fairly affectionate with my mother—but the rules are different between men and boys and men and men. The kind of crying I'm talking about is the unabashed kind, from wide-open weeping to sob-your-guts-out. Tearing up a bit during a sappy movie, the little catch in the throat when recalling or recounting a death or a loss—that kind of crying doesn't really count. Moviemakers, TV writers, book writers—most of them can make us cry a little. Hell, it's an industry.

I wanted to hear some crying stories. I wanted to hear about sobbing, weeping, wailing, blubbering, puling. The kind of crying after which, or in conjunction with, there arise ululations. The problem is: How am I going to get people, particularly men, particularly tough men, macho men, to talk about it? It turns out all I had to do was ask—sometimes. Sometimes that worked.

But before I hit the streets and the phone to try to scare up customers, I thought I should know something about the science of tears—their composition, tear ducts, the mechanics, why they exist at all. We know that tears, or teary secretions, keep the eyeballs clean and lubricated. I have a friend with an eye problem. His eyes, at night, don't do this. Therefore, he wakes up with his eyelid glued to his eyeball. This, he tells me, is disconcerting, as well as very painful. He's solved the problem with eye drops just before bed as well as scotch-taping his eye shut (a part of his treatment not prescribed by his ophthalmologist). But what else are tears intended for? What purpose do they have—physically? Later, too, I hoped to learn something about what purpose they serve psychologically, the science of which I knew would be less, well, scientific.

The tear duct and gland: Also known as the lachrymal duct and gland. I prefer the lachrymal, even though I rarely prefer a polysyllabic word when a one-syllable word does just as well. I like the sound of the word, its tumbling, dactylic rhythm: Stress, unstressed, unstressed. I like that it begins and ends with the sweet consonant "l," that it contains, early, the harsh and nasal *ack* sound, which is then softened by the smoother and vibrating "r" and "m" sounds. I like the tears of Christ association. I grew up Episcopalian and always envied my Catholic pals who could brag about the nuns beating the crap out of them and brag, too, about all the serious and complex sins they had to watch out for—some only venal, some mortal. I always felt being Episcopalian was like being Junior Varsity to the Catholic Varsity. So: "Lachrymal" it will be.

These structures, make, distribute, and then remove tears. The basic job of tears is to moisten the membrane, called the conjunctiva, which covers our eyeballs and facilitates motion. This thin film over our eyes keeps them moist and will float irritants—dust, minute traces of nuclear fallout, pollutants, and the smallest swirling orts—off our eyeballs. Blinking keeps the tears spread evenly, smoothly.

Lachrymal glands start working extra at the sign of particular and less common irritants: Onion fumes, eating a hot pepper, heavy smoke. Powered-up tears like these are called "reflex" or "irritant" tears. More later about the other kind of tears, called, appropriately, "emotional" tears. Lachrymal glands are almond shaped and extend from under the upper eyelids inward from the far corner of each eye. I have also heard them described as looking like a "shelled walnut" because they are in two sections. One is a shallow depression in the part of the eye socket formed by the frontal bone. The other part projects into the back of the upper lid. I have a feeling that scientists, using nut similes to describe lachrymal glands, are on to something, but I'm not sure what. If I find more nut metaphors or similes in other research on this apparatus, I will investigate further. The lachrymal glands have three to twelve openings into the superior conjunctival sac: A bag of tears. And from here, the tears flow down the eye and across the eye into the *puncta lacrimalia*, small openings at the edge of each eyelid near the inner corner. The *puncta* open into the lachrymal ducts (a word I like less than glands—it sounds vaguely agricultural, where at least glands have sexual connotations), which open to lachrymal sacs, which are the squeezed upper-end of the nasolachrymal ducts, which carry the tears into the nose, which is why crying is so often accompanied by prodigious nose-blowing.

I must digress for a few moments to tell you about something else that might pass through tear ducts and emerge from the corners of one's eye: A maw-worm. A maw-worm is a parasite, similar to a tape worm, growing up to thirty centimeters (seven to eight inches!) long, that migrates inside the body (including in the lungs and liver) and occasionally exits the body (where it thinks it's going, I don't know) via various orifices, "including, most alarmingly, the corners of people's eyes." Not to worry though—unless you visit certain islands in the Malaysian archipelago, this parasite is rare.

Why don't the tears evaporate as they wash across the eyeball? That's the question everyone is asking. Other glands produce oily and mucous substances, which prevent this and also, when deposited at the bottom eyelid margins, act as a kind of dam to keep normal tears from spilling out. They divert the tears to the above-mentioned lachrymal ducts. Pretty goddamn efficient. Unless you have Sjogren's Syndrome, known more commonly as Dry Eye Syndrome. Perhaps this is what my friend has, or a version of it. People with this problem must use artificial tears to moisten their eyes, as often as every ten or fifteen minutes. For some irrational reason, perhaps similar to medical students convincing themselves they've contracted the rare disease they're studying, I decide never to visit Sweden. Infants, who cry a lot, don't develop the lachrymal gland until they're six or eight weeks old: They cry without weeping. Maybe they have Sjorgren Junior's Syndrome, which hurts, which is why they cry.

I needed to hear some crying stories. My interviewing technique would be simple: When was the last time you cried your guts out and why? I'd also ask people if they ever saw their father cry.

Susan B., early fifties, runs her husband's medical office: "I was at the office, working, opening mail. Took out a blue report (always from the Nuclear Medicine Department). They print their reports on both sides of the sheet, and I opened it to the second side, where it has the part of the report that says 'Conclusions.' It said their tests had confirmed the patient has cancer in twenty-six different parts of the body, and listed all twenty-six places. Inoperable, terminal, less than two months to live. I kept saying as I read it: Oh, this poor patient! and then I turned it over and it had my mother's name at the top. I let out a wail that was like a sound I'd never heard before. We weren't having office hours, fortunately, at that time, so I went into the first examining room and closed the door and sobbed. Wailing, for all the world to hear, banging my fist on the examining table, crying all over the white paper we pull down so it's nice and fresh for the next patient. I couldn't stop the waves of sobs. Finally, Pat (one of the women in the office) came back and knocked on the door, afraid to open it. They had no idea what had happened because I just got up from my desk and walked away, unable to talk. I handed her the report, which was smeared and wet by now. She read it and sat down next to me and cried. She loved my mother too. She lived long enough to be present and a part of Eric's (her grandson) Bar Mitzvah celebration and after that wonderful day, never got dressed, never was able to speak. She made it through three months before she died. And I never cried once. For me, it was learning that her death was certain and coming soon that made me cry, and the cruel shock of finding out the way I did. I was mourning her loss, my friend before all others, that day in the examining room, and recognized it for that. From then on, all I wanted to do was enjoy my time with her. I cried it all out, and got on with making her comfortable and as happy as possible. She never could stand to see me cry." I love that previous sentence. It sums up Susan's character: Again, as in all through her story, it is others' needs that come first. I asked her if she ever saw her father cry. She said no, but described a scene for me: Her father and mother were separating. Susan and her brother stood on the steps of the house. The father was driving away. Their mother was behind them looking out a window. They didn't want to wave openly goodbye to their father because they thought this would upset their mother. They waved with their arms tucked into their chests so the mother couldn't see them but the father could. That image almost made me cry.

Francis Hepburn was the first man I talked to. I heard the only time he cried in his life (as an adult) was just after WWII when he was mustered out of the Marines and had to give his rifle back—the standard issue M-1 Garand—which literally had not been out of arm's length for over two years. Francis is seventy-seven, about six feet tall, trim, and handsome. He never removed a white cap as we talked. (When I met him again, a few months later, he wasn't wearing the cap, and I almost didn't recognize him. He has a full head of hair.) We sat at the coffee bar in the San Diego Amtrak Station. He's originally from New Mexico but has lived in San Diego since just after the war. He was a Marine Raider and saw about two years of some of the heaviest combat in the Pacific. He took part in amphibious assaults in the Solomons and fought the whole length of Okinawa, landing, eerily unopposed, as part of Operation Iceberg, in April of 1945. The opposition and the slaughter began a few days later. Over 12,000 American soldiers died. Well over 100,000 Japanese soldiers and civilians died. It was the carnage on Okinawa that helped push Truman towards dropping atomic bombs on the Japanese mainland. Okinawa is where many civilians, told the Americans would rape and torture them, jumped off cliffs to their deaths—women, children, old people—while American soldiers tried to talk them out of it. You've seen the newsreel footage if you're over fifty.

His closest call came on Okinawa: A Japanese mortar shell, most likely from a small mortar/grenade launcher (sometimes called a "knee mortar") the Japanese used with especial accuracy, and which American troops feared, hit the lip of his foxhole. He was knocked unconscious, probably had a concussion, and was given a shot of morphine. It rained all night—he's still unconscious in his foxhole. He wakes up in water up to his chest, and his first thought is: My rifle! It was there, underwater like him all night, and he was relieved when he cleaned it up that it still worked. He lived through Okinawa, and in September 1945, he was among the first Americans to land in Japan after the unconditional surrender. And he was one of the first Americans to go AWOL in Japan. On their first night, he and a buddy saw lights and heard voices, music, a few hundred yards away from where they were setting up camp. They decided to check it out and were not disappointed to find some whiskey and some female companionship. He said, rather sheepishly, that he believes he might have been the first American soldier to get drunk in occupied Japan. A little twinkle and a slightly arched eyebrow (his wife was nearby) implied that the whiskey was not the only first that night.

When we talked in the train station, Francis gestured with his thumb over his shoulder: "It was right over there," he said, meaning the place where he was kicked free of the Marines. He'd been stateside four of five days when he heard an announcement over a loudspeaker: Line up at such-and-such building, and bring your 782 gear: Pack, tents, cartridge belts, weapons, etc. He remembers a long table. And a man behind it—a stateside soldier, outranking him. Francis left the marines a Pfc.—he'd lost a stripe for the little incident in Tokyo. The Corporal said "Gimme your rifle." Francis saw a huge pile of them behind the man. "Like hell I will!" said Francis. My rifle, he thought, stacked like wood, no! The soldier behind the table was a little nervous by now. He called an officer over. The officer said to Francis: "Didn't you know you had to hand over your rifle?" Francis was starting to panic. The officer told him he wasn't getting out until he turned it over. He handed it over. The Corporal tossed it in the pile. Francis lunged over the table—to get his rifle back, to strangle the man who took it—he wasn't quite sure. He had heard someone say he's gone "Asiatic"—meaning he'd been over there too long. "It was like someone had said to me: 'Give me your arm.'" Eventually, he calmed down, a kind of compromise was reached: They'd let him keep his knife. He finally walked outside, further away from his rifle than he'd been in years, and "I just looked around and burst into tears." Never cried before, during or after combat. "This was the only time," he said, and as he told me, a small sob rolled out of his chest, and his eyes teared-up. He said: "I've learned since then that tears are controllable. I've been to lots of cemeteries." His wife, Eloise, had joined us at the table about halfway through our talk. She said to me, after Francis had gone ahead to get their car, "I was very moved hearing him talk to you like that. To be honest, I've learned something today that helps me to understand him." She already knew his crying story. In fact, she first mentioned it to me and talked him into talking to me. She meant his whole demeanor, his vulnerability, what he'd been through. I could see him disappearing across the wide station. A few weeks later he wrote to me: "The tears I shed when they took my rifle were not tears of mourning, but rather of great frustration, anger, and peevishness like a baby when a pacifier is pulled out of his mouth." He's a man whose hand I'm glad I had the opportunity to shake.

I heard about a woman who got kicked out of movies because she cried so much and so loud. Her name is Lisa, she's twenty-nine, and works in San Diego with troubled teenagers. I asked her about getting kicked out of movies—the image of someone half-led, half-dragged out of a movie theater by two guys with flashlights and wearing bellhop suits refused to leave my mind. What would a member of the audience do? Watch that scene or the screen? Lisa indicated that getting kicked out of the movies might be a bit hyperbolic on the part of her friends. She said she has to sometimes walk herself out. She then added, "I do sometimes cry at previews." She said (I heard this a few times, from men and women): "I laugh hard, I cry hard." I thought of something the great Russian writer Maxim Gorky said when asked why he wept upon hearing a poem recited: "That's how my eyes are made. Happiness moves me to tears (and then added apologetically), but I feel unhappiness in silence."

Lisa does not feel unhappiness in silence. And when she cries, it's not just tears rolling down her face, no, it's "sobbing, bawling to the point where I can barely breathe, my eyes swell up, once for nearly two days." She grew up in New Jersey, and her parents were divorced when she was one. "There was a lot of crying going on there," she said, laughing. She told me she sometimes wakes up crying from a dream. She's Catholic and cries when she prays. She has a younger sister, but her family always called her "the baby" anyway. She told me she was reading *Angela's Ashes* and crying even over semi-colons and commas. I exaggerate this last, but I kept thinking: What great human emotional honesty, how wonderful to express feelings in such an open way. And, at the same time thinking: This could really be embarrassing, walking with her and she sees a dead pigeon and all of a sudden she's caterwauling right there on the sidewalk! People look at you and think: What did you do to make that poor woman cry so? All the while she talked to me, Lisa was upbeat, energetic, and all the while we talked, I was afraid she'd cry.

The science of tears goes well beyond the mere physiological apparatus, and new studies explore the relationship between suppressed tears and particular stress-associated illnesses and between the free release of tears and health. Margaret Crepeau, at the University of Pittsburgh School of Nursing did the first studies in this area in 1979. It did not surprise me that a woman and a nurse was the first person to try to document this connection. Common sense, empirical knowledge, and even doctors—Dr. Lucille Peszat, for example, calls it "a chemical wash"—tell us crying is good for us. Dr. Peszat is referring to the combination of water, salt, protein, lipids, and sugar of which our tears are made. That we always feel better after a good cry. Uh-huh. Men give this notion lip service. Research confirms this: Only 63% of men say they feel better after a good cry. Eighty-five percent of women report feeling better. There should be a dating service that matches that 27% of men with that 15% of women. Those that married would make good and quiet neighbors until one of them eventually popped a cork and bludgeoned the other to death with a Garden Weasel. "Our bodies will produce signals indicating stress until we deal with the underlying reason," Dr. Peszat says.

Dr. William Frey, a biochemist and a nationally-recognized tear expert agrees. He says people can handle low-level frustration all of the time, but when "the intensity of emotion crosses the barrier, we cry." He reports that women cry 5.3 times a month, which seems to me, empirically, about right. And which explains why a woman with whom I once lived would seem to cry five or six times each month, and why, one month, when she didn't cry for over three weeks, she then cried for five days in a row and then on the last day of the month started weeping inconsolably but stopped about 70% sooner than she usually did. Frey reports that men cry, on average, 1.4 times a month. Not one man I spoke to admitted crying almost one and one-half times a month. I mean *crying*, not eyes moistening a bit, or even a few tears rolling down. As I said at the onset: That doesn't count. That happened to me three times recently while watching a dog movie with my daughter!

Here's another interesting statistic: Most people cry between 7 and 10 P.M. That's when we spend the most time with our families, our significant others. Big surprise there. It's also a time when we're more tired, we have more privacy, and then there are always the tearjerkers on TV. Crying, Frey believes, is nature's way of relieving stress: "It does relieve stress, although it's not entirely known exactly how it works." He thinks that crying removes chemicals that build up during stress. In fact, his studies have shown that tears shed in response to emotional pain have a higher protein content than tears shed as a result of mere eye irritation. His tests shows that not all tears are the same but "don't show why they're different," said Frey. Frey and some others also think that tears are another way the body rids itself of waste, in a sense not much different than urinating or defecating. If this is so, it's a tiny, complicated apparatus designed to remove—in comparison—an insignificant amount of body waste: About 1.1 grams a day, about 1/28 of an ounce. A mouse must evacuate that much waste a day, and I don't know if they cry. Dr. Peszat says, "Crying is not a weakness or a bad thing." She also says excessive or chronic weeping can be a signal of clinical depression.

Another expert, Dr. Marc George, has found that normal grief (which he recreated in the laboratory by having patients recall painful memories) produces a pattern of brain metabolism very similar to that in patients who are clinically depressed. Weeping gets rid of chemicals in our bodies that depress us? Prozac, et al, gives our bodies the ability to make certain chemicals, the lack of which cause depression? Would our best chance at happiness mean crying a lot and taking Prozac? That seems to me to cover all the bases.

I thought talking to some people in prison about crying might be a good idea. Does much crying go on in prison? What are the rules? I made a call to a friend who teaches in a prison. A week or so later I got a call from a guy, Jack, in his early forties, doing hard time at a maximum-security prison. I knew he was calling from there because I had to accept collect charges, and the operator said the call came from such-and-such correctional facility. The nature of his offense did not arise. I asked him if guys cry in the joint. He said that by the time guys got to where he is (max), they've been inside a while and are not likely to be blubbering too much. It would be a sign of weakness. I could hear a general din behind him with an occasional single voice rising above it—prisons are always noisy. I asked him right out: When's the last time you cried in there and why? I didn't ask him if, I just asked him when. I had lulled him a little bit by asking about guys in the joint in general. He said: "Last night. My kids." And then I heard a kind of stuttering, the kind wrenched from the chest, the lungs, the deep belly—uh,uh,uh,uh—shortened, squashed, fought-against sobs. Very quiet, below his normal voice just moments before, uh,uh,uh,uh. Then he hung up. I didn't get a chance to ask him if he'd ever seen his father cry.

I got some calls from women in prison. This time it was a medium-security place where the inmates were serving sentences of up to a year or were waiting to be sent upstate for longer stretches. The first woman I talked to was Stacey, in her late thirties. I asked her why, under what circumstances women cry in prison. She, like Jack, said, "My children." And as she said it, she started to cry. She said her mom raises her children "because I don't know how to stop doing drugs." I asked her if there were treatment options. She said: "AA, once a week." Then she said she didn't belong in jail because she was an addict. She made the argument that addiction is an illness, which is true, of course, but one is still responsible for one's actions, addicted or not. I said something like this to her. She stopped crying. She said, "There's another woman here who wants to talk to you." The phone dangled for a while—I heard it knock against the wall a few times, heard a similar din but a little more high-pitched than in the man's joint, then Melinda (she happily gave me her last name, but I've decided to write this, with one exception, without them). She made sure I got that her name was Melinda and not Belinda. She's forty-eight years old, and this is her story. Many years ago she was convicted of manslaughter. She said it was a "domestic abuse situation." When she failed to elaborate, I said: "Do you mean you killed someone who was abusing you in a relationship?" She said: "Correct." Melinda did nearly a dime for that. She had two small children at the time. She'd been out a few years when, pulled over for a routine traffic stop, the cops found some marijuana in her car. That cost her three months back in the joint. When she began serving this, she brought some Extra Strength Tylenol with her, as she described: "On my person." For this—they contained codeine—she got another nine months: Bingo, back in the bing for a year.

I asked Melinda about other women crying inside. She said most do it in private, when they're locked up alone at night. And sometimes it's remorse, or missing kids, and sometimes fears: "What if there's a fire, I'm locked in here. What if somebody had an asthma attack? That happens a lot. What if the guard's in the bathroom and there's a fire?" I wasn't sure where she was going with this: I hadn't heard of many prison fires; most are made out of concrete and steel. She told me there was a lot of crying going on at church services in prison. But not sobbing, the tears rolling down the face "and then they're wiped away quickly." She told a story that happened that day. A young woman, new to jail, new to this block (there are twenty-six women in each block) was acting up, kicking a door, making a ruckus, and she got locked down for this, at which point she started really wailing and sobbing. Melinda said a lot of the women were laughing at her, making fun of her, but more in a veteran vs. rookie kind of way: "Look at this dumb kid, she don't know what's gonna happen to her for acting like this." Then she said when the young woman got out of lockup the next morning, everyone will be friendly and supportive, like she'd passed some sort of initiation. I asked Melinda (I knew I had a live one) about visiting times and could children come at any age. Yes—from infants on up. But this was the hard part: Parents and children could embrace but only across a table. Each had to stay on their side. A child can't sit on her mother's lap. Older children didn't like this but can understand it; whereas, a toddler can't understand why he can't crawl across that table! After those meetings—that's when women often go to their cells and close themselves in. Finally, Melinda was ready to tell me a personal story about the last time she really lost it in prison. She said it was right after she was sentenced to the extra nine months on top of the three she already had to do, and she looked at her first meal back inside. "I looked at the food and I cried. I was hungry, and I knew I had to eat it, but it was so horrible, and I cried and cried and got locked down in the forensic block (the psych block) because they thought I was going crazy." As of this writing (March 2000), Melinda is due to get out on June 9th. She says the only thing that might make her cry then is "the unknown."

Most of the men I talked to about crying wanted to relate a concept, an image. One of my friends immediately thought of "the tears that come to your eyes when you're riding your bicycle down a hill on a cold day." It was a good image. But did he have any good crying stories himself? No. Another friend, a journalist, had the concept: "What about tears that can kill?" I said, "Huh?" He said: "AIDS, does an AIDS or an HIV-positive person's tears have the potential to infect another person with the virus?" He was struck by the horror of that if it were true—that one's tears shared with a loved one might possibly infect that loved one. He's about to go undercover as a journalist and present himself as an AIDS patient at certain hospital emergency rooms where he's been told that real AIDS patients, particularly homeless AIDS patients, are treated badly. So how about a crying story from him? Nope, nada, pal. A few people (men) I asked offered to quote some poetry—Tennyson, Keats—poets who can make me cry, they said. I said, I don't want to cry, I want to hear stories, especially stories by men, since it's harder to get men to talk about it, and they say, "Right, it's harder to talk about it." "So?" I say. Two of them, a few days apart, one in person and one on the phone, said: "So fucking what?" Which means, with an italicized *what*: End of conversation regarding crying.

OK, crying's good for you. Cleanses the body of toxins. Unless you cry too much. Then you embarrass yourself or other people. Or you get sent to the psych ward. Crying relieves stress. I like that word: "Stress." It's a word that, metrically, would almost always get a stress. I like the adjective/noun combination "stress test." A rhyming spondee.

My guess is Francis Hepburn and all those other eighteen- and nineteen-year-old soldiers never heard that word "stress." "Men," says the Captain, "it's going to be a little stressful out there today." Francis told me there was a particular kind of very common poisonous snake on Okinawa (called locally *habu*) that "we often had to fight in." So here are guys constantly getting shot at, howitzers, mortars, crazy motherfucking Japanese soldiers happy to die, coming at them with everything they've got, and these guys are fighting "in" snakes! Stress! He told me they often licked their cartridge clips clean of mud before the clip would slide in their rifles. He told me that on Guam, under heavy machine gun fire, he jumped in a shell hole and noticed he was standing in something unpleasantly squishy. Turns out it was a Japanese corpse. It bothered him that the stuff got all over his pants. And then there were mosquitoes, so many he could barely breathe. Stress? He found a new hole.

What's that new drug for shyness? I wonder if army shrinks

then were working on a drug that allayed fears of a viper planting its needles behind your knees while, at the same time, chunks of razor-sharp metal are whizzing beneath your chin and you're standing in corpses up to your knees!

Francis Hepburn and his colleagues were at work. They were on the job. And that's where stress most often occurs in our lives. Ergo: A lot of crying goes on in the workplace and is acceptable there? Don't think so. Is the unacceptability thereof why the Post Office has occasional problems with highly-stressed employees who have no opportunity to weep on the job?

I run into tears, sometimes, in my line of work, teaching. A few weeks ago a young Asian-American man sat in my office and told me a story about his father's boss making fun of his father's accent—he'd come to America as a young man from Taiwan. My student was a small boy when he saw his father humiliated. As he spoke, large runnels of tears came from each eye. He didn't make a sound. As I've said: These kinds of tears don't really count, but this seemed to me an exception. Tears rose in my eyes too. Maybe that's the exception: Two men brought to tears over the sadness of one of them. I told him it took a brave man to cry in front of another man. I meant that. I'm not sure he felt the same way.

I talked to a woman friend who works in an office of all women, seven or eight of them. She told me after several months together, their periods and PMS times all became coordinated, and particularly during PMS, there's a lot of weeping, enough that they laugh about it. I tried to picture an office of seven or eight men doing something even remotely similar, and all that came into my mind were the words "insufficient data."

Barbara Reinhold has written a book called *Toxic Work: How to Overcome Stress, Burnout, and Revitalize Your Career.* Ms. Reinhold is Director of Career Development at Smith College in Northampton, MA. This happens to be, coincidentally, a few miles from where I grew up, and where my parents still live. My mother, in her last decade or so before retiring, worked as the night switchboard operator at the Northampton State Hospital, formerly one of Massachusetts' largest public mental hospitals.

It's now closed. This hospital is only about a half a mile from the Smith College campus. In fact, the Smith College riding team practiced its jumps and dressage exercises on property that abutted the hospital grounds. I say this not only because of the small-world coincidence of it, but also because stress seems to be the cause of a lot of mental breakdowns. My mother often reported a patient brought into the hospital, strapped to a gurney, raving. Most of the time she would add, "And he had long hair like you, Tommy." This was the early 70s. I could never see the correlation of mental health and long hair, but one must never underestimate the almost preternatural powers of mothers.

Ms. Reinhard also heads her own employment-consulting firm and knows a lot of women executives who admit to crying on the job. She has one major piece of advice—be discreet: "You have to know how to sob over the sink without messing up your eye makeup…it's important to have that release, but not to look as though you've been crying." How to sob over the sink without messing up your eye makeup! The older I get the more and more women amaze me and the clearer it gets that they are superior beings! I am dead serious. Reinhard warns that crying at the workplace reinforces stereotypical views of women and also shuts down communication: "The single most important thing anybody needs in the workplace is feedback. What you're going to do by crying is essentially throw away the possibility that people will talk straight to you." She quotes a woman named Delores: "There were a couple of years in the early 90s when I was severely overworked, always dead tired and completely burned out. On a couple of occasions, I retreated to the women's restroom and cried. Never in front of co-workers." Delores was doing actuarial work at the time. (There, I thought, was something to make me cry too!) She said tears at the office could be seen as a sign of weakness—not unlike in prison, I thought.

Is it gonna get touchy-feely in the office? Unlikely, thinks Thomas Anastasi, an instructor at the Boston University School of Management and an expert in controversial work behavior: "If anything, it makes things worse. Any type of emotional display—

joy, sorrow, laughing—is frowned upon. People are expected to be even-keeled. It's just easier to not deal with emotions on the job." Anastasi quotes a man named Tom. Tom was a manager for a major supermarket chain, and one of the people who worked for him cried: "I always found it goofy. I can understand grief. But being overwhelmed about a temporary situation at work, I just think that person needs to be in a less stressful job, maybe filing books at the library." His word choice, "goofy," is absolutely male. Most men are just flat-out baffled by this kind of emotionality—it seems, in fact, like cartoon behavior. And, in case you missed Tom's final point: Men who cry on the job are like women, i.e., librarians. Tom may be a bit of an insensitive lout, but he's being honest. How does Tom deal with stress? "I get up and walk away for fifteen or twenty minutes." How sane. How rational. "But to cry," said Tom, "I don't see how that's productive." Tom is one of the original Tom, Dick, and Harries—an everyman and his brother.

It's time for a few more crying stories, just the human business, everybody's got a story, and how did Tolstoy put it? All happy families are happy in the same way and are boring. All unhappy families are unhappy in different ways and, therefore, not boring. That's a rather loose translation, but I believe covers the spirit of Tolstoy's law.

One woman I talked to, Eloise H., gave me a visual image of this law with her hand—she held it up with the thumb tucked in and said, "Place the index finger and middle finger snug together and you have my mother and my sister's relationship, separate the ring finger distant and you find my father. From there the little finger stretches over the horizon and you find me." There were tears in this hand signal.

Emmy J. went to a psychiatrist to learn how to cry. As an adult. As a child, she was not allowed to cry. She still did so, sometimes, silently, but it released, relieved nothing. Both her parents and grandparents disapproved of emotionality. Her grandmother told her, when her own sons were small: "You're not raising schoolgirls, you're raising boys." About her father she said two things: "No bawling!" (He said this.) And that she always felt "under his microscope." Take a guess: Had she ever seen her father cry? She then added that both her parents were dead, and "I had no closure with either of them." She decided to do something about her own inability to cry when her sons got older and had some trouble at school. She sought the help of a therapist and told her story. The therapist said: "Why aren't you crying?" Emmy said: "I am." The therapist suggested she continue dropping by the office. She joined a group. She gained a sense of permission, for the first time in her life, to cry, and she felt safe to do so. She was even taught techniques in how to start crying and to keep it going (quitting too soon is maybe worse than not crying at all). "When you cry, push it out and then you suck it all back in again, inhale, cry, exhale, inhale, cry, exhale, keep on, pumping the well dry." How is crying different now? "It's a relief, a release, not carrying around a pressure cooker with a lid on." Emmy admitted to being a closet poet. I thought of some lines of Tennyson's: "Home they brought her warrior dead./She nor swooned nor uttered cry;/All her maidens, watching, said,/She must weep or she will die."

I have a friend, Marc S., who is an oncologist and a poet. He has a large practice and specializes in last-ditch chemo treatment. All else fails: Come to him, and he puts together the different kinds of poisons in the right combinations to battle the cancer. It's his particular skill: Which drugs, what combinations, what doses, which must be just below what would kill you by themselves. He uses the word "cure." Sometimes. He's seen patients cry. He's cried on the job and medical personnel (76% of nurses, 57% of doctors, and 31% of medical students) admit to doing so too. I assume the reason medical students cry less is because the suffering they've seen is, so far, minimal. Marc is a gifted poet, published two books with a very reputable press, and writes many of his poems in the voices of patients as well as doctors. He writes a lot about what he knows, what he sees, and what he sees a lot of is death and the horrible and courageous battles fought to hold it off a little longer. Did he have a story about crying himself? Nope. But this is what he told me: "Last week a thirty-eight-year-old woman came to my office with a newly-diagnosed breast cancer that had been growing at a raging rate. We sat for over two hours while I discussed biology, treatment options, prognosis, especially my belief that she required an aggressive approach. All the while her husband and mother were present—he occasionally asking academic-type questions, having run through internet sources for two days. But it was her mother who surprised. She sat quietly and asked nothing and looking slightly away, so it was hard for me to see her face and impossible for her daughter. Finally, I understood why. She was crying the whole time, soundless, without taking out a telltale tissue and with as much pain as I can remember. I have rarely seen such profound crying so long and so silent." Marc diagnosed and treated his own father's pancreatic cancer. He didn't have a crying story for that.

Meredith K. has rules for crying. What she calls "an intelligent approach to crying." Paramount: "Don't let them see you cry. Otherwise they win." She recalled an incident as a teenager when she was punished unfairly for something and flat out refused to cry. She spoke with derision of a boss in an office where she used to work. Whenever an employee entered his office to discuss a performance report, he made a point of opening his drawer and pulling out a box of tissues as the employee sat down. He'd make a show of it, saying nothing and then beginning the discussion. Some people would break into tears on the spot. Emmy resented this intimidation technique. She thought it gratuitously cruel. It never worked with her. I asked her where she'd cry. She said, "In the car, alone." Sometimes she'll cry in the shower at the gym. That struck me as pretty clever. Meredith grew up in Fresno and Imperial Beach in a mixed family, parents divorced, remarried, stepbrothers and -sisters. Her mother had some mental problems: "Mother played out most of the emotion of the family—she used up her share and everybody else's." Meredith has two grown daughters herself and realized that she taught them not to cry. This horrified her. Then, over a ten-year period, several members of her family died, some in terrible ways—plane, car, motorcycle crashes. Her father died. Her mother, still alive, has Alzheimer's. Meredith takes care of her. During all these deaths, Meredith was in charge of everything. She said: "I would not say I've learned to grieve well." She did take a ten-week course in grief counseling. She said it was "helpful, from an intelligent point of view, in understanding the process of grief, to learn how others grieve." She reads a lot of philosophy rather than poetry, about fifty books a year. The last thing she said to me was: "I'm interested in what we forget."

Was it implicit when this began that before it was over I'd tell my own crying story? When was the last time I cried my guts out? Ain't nobody's bidness but my own.

Norman Ottomar Lux

My father, a milkman, went to work 6,206 days in a row, give or take a few, from 1945 until 1962. Until I was sixteen and my cousin, Jackie, eighteen or nineteen. We were both old enough to drive the milk truck then, and we knew his routes, since we'd been (I speak for myself) half-assed helpers of his. So he took his first days off in seventeen years. He and my mother went away somewhere, and my cousin and I delivered the milk for a week. As far as I know, no baby died for lack of it: We made the rounds, Jackie and I, up and down the streets of our small town—Elm and Cottage and Clark—sometime during the summer of 1962.

My father divided his customers into two routes, one Monday/Wednesday/Friday, and the other Tuesday/Thursday. On Saturdays he did both. On Sundays he delivered to three or four stores. He slept in a bit on Sundays, but he still shaped up for work. My mother worked too, full-time, as a telephone operator, as well as acting as primary caretaker of her aging and increasingly-ill mother, my grandmother, with whom we lived, on the family farm. My grandfather, the last life-long farmer in the family, died when I was three. My uncle (mother's side) milked the cows. My father delivered it. During crunch times, haying, for example, everybody helped. The point is: They went to work. You did this: You went to work. Glad to have a job—they went through the Depression and then, right on its back, came WWII. You go to work: That's a great lesson, for which I am grateful.

My father liked his job. He was, essentially, his own boss. He loaded his truck in the morning and came back with empty bottles at night. Sometimes, in grade school, he'd drive by when we were out for recess or at lunch. That filled me with joy. I helped him on Saturdays, his double route. He'd pick me up about 10:30, letting me sleep late. I learned some very useful things working with him. One: How to drive a truck, which, after I graduated from college, I did for a while to earn a living. And two: A sense of balance. I could stand next to him (large, stand-up front cab to allow easy and frequent exit and entry) and, without holding on to anything, not lose my balance as he went around corners, stopped quickly, etc. I can ride New York City subways without holding a pole—a kind of urban surfing.

People paid for their milk with little blue tickets. They'd leave him some money, he'd leave the blue tickets, and then they'd give him back the tickets for milk. He carried a little sack of the cash—maybe twenty to thirty dollars in bills and another twenty in change. For this sack of change, which he hung up in the laundry room off the kitchen after work, I am also grateful. In my teen years, I'd clip a buck or so in dimes and quarters for a few gallons of gas with which to cruise with my pals in my parents' or their parents' cars. My bet is he knew I was skimming now and then from the family business—I think he could tell, by the heft of it, just how much change was in his sack. Good trick (let them *think* they're getting away with something, sometimes) to use on kids, Pop, thanks. I use the same trick on your granddaughter. And I taught her the one song you taught me: "Oh, the monkey chased his tail around the flag pole"—one line, over and over. It fills us both with joy. Thank you, Father, your genius was your heart, and you taught me more than you knew.

Norman O. Lux (1915–2010)

About the Author

Thomas Lux was born in December 1946. He has been awarded fellowships from the Guggenheim Foundation, the Mellon Foundation, and three times from the NEA. He received the Kingsley Tufts Award for his book *Split Horizon*. His most recent collection of poems is *God Particles* (Houghton Mifflin, 2008), and Houghton Mifflin Harcourt will publish *Child Made of Sand* in 2012. Lux is Bourne Professor of Poetry and Director of the McEver Visiting Writers Program at the Georgia Institute of Technology, and is a frequent visitor to the MFA programs at Sarah Lawrence College and Warren Wilson College. He lives in Atlanta.

www.ingramcontent.com/pod-product-compliance
Lightning Source LLC
LaVergne TN
LVHW011417080426
835512LV00005B/117